The Warrior Wives Club:
Fighting For Your Marriage One Week at a Time

By:

Ashby Duval

First Electronic Edition: 2019
First Print Edition: 2019

Dedication:

To the Warrior Wives, without whom this book would not exist.
You inspired me every week as you fought for your marriages and
the marriages of the other women in our group with the power
of prayer and the truth of God's word. This journey with you has
changed my life and marriage for the better.

TABLE OF CONTENTS

INTRODUCTION

You may think I'm writing this because I've got my act together but I'm going to burst your bubble right off the bat. I was married less than two years when the Lord put this group on my heart to start. Three years and over 100 marriages changed later, the adventure He took us on was too amazing to not share with others. Looking back, I think this journey began in my first marriage before I was suddenly widowed at the age of 26. I never wanted to get married until I met Spencer and once I did, I so badly wanted it to last that I went around asking people for their best marriage advice. Spencer's mom was actually the one who gave me my favorite and most applicable wisdom ever: "weed your own garden." She made the point that we have enough of our own issues to last a lifetime, so work on YOUR problems with the Lord instead of focusing on your husband's. She and my sweet father "in love" (they refused to call me an in-law but an in-love!) have been married 40 plus years and help lead a marriage ministry called 2equal1 in many countries. Needless to say, her advice was well received.

When Spencer died suddenly of an enlarged heart fifteen months into our marriage, I was completely devastated. On top of that, I was five months pregnant with our first son. I genuinely never wanted to get married again but thankfully Jesus had other plans. When Dominic and I met four years later, Spencer's parents were so supportive and flew all of us to Minnesota for my birthday so they could meet him. When we were getting married a year after that, they told me they weren't losing a daughter but gaining a son and welcomed him with open arms. They had been praying for him after all! And my three year old son Trooper had been praying too for a "daddy on earth" so you can imagine the kind of special man God brought into my life. Right before we were married, I asked for a refresher in marriage advice and she brought this point up again. It's had a huge impact on my life and the more I spoke with others, the more I realized how this could help their marriages as well.

One day I was speaking with a friend about her struggling marriage and she told me she had read about a group of women who started praying together for their marriages regularly and the incredible impact it had. When I hung up, I knew I needed to start my own prayer group with the premise that we need to "weed our own gardens" and focus on praying for our husbands instead of trying to change them. The idea was so vividly specific that I immediately called my best friend to see what she thought and asked if she would be interested. She was not only interested but she enthusiastically offered her home which was much more conducive to a group meeting than mine. My heart was beating so fast and I knew I needed to send an email inviting others to join as soon as possible. The conviction was so strong I felt if I had waited until even an hour later, it would be unwise. Less than a handful of times in my life have I ever felt so perfectly certain about something and *never* had I had such an instantly clear overview of how something should look. Grabbing my computer, I prayed for God to bring to mind women to invite and to give me the words for the email. Within minutes, I had a group of 20 or so women in mind and sent this exact email:

Hi Ladies,

I had an idea I wanted to run by you. Right before I got married, God put a theme in my life that started with my sweet mother "in love" giving me advice: "Pray it on him, don't lay it on him." "Weed your own garden" were the wise words of a woman who has been happily married for 40 years.

Now I wish I could say I took those words and ran with them... but (per usual) I've been learning by trial and error and God in His sweet and merciful fashion has had to drive the point home to me in many different ways. Long story short, I'm finally starting to see how powerful praying over your husband can be ESPECIALLY before just saying whatever I think he needs to hear. The beautiful thing is that in this journey, I feel like Jesus is transforming MY heart even more than his. Who knew I was just as much of the problem?! Lol

Hence you find me with a proposition: *Warrior Wives Club*. We would meet once a month at Kate's house and I would send you an email once a week with scripture and topics for praying over our spouses. At our monthly meeting, I would try and line up a speaker of a trusted older woman who has some wisdom to pass on to us younger gals on marriage, a sermon or some sort of marriage related video. For example, a lady from our church this past Sunday who has been married for 60 years (yes! 60!) said that in addition to praying regularly for her husband and children, she found that being positive and joyful (joyful with her hubby, joyful raising her kids, just a general joyful attitude) is one of the things she would suggest to other wives. Not being negative but encouraging is extremely powerful. We would end with prayer of course but would be respectful of everyone's time and would try and keep the monthly meeting to two hours or less.

PLEASE DON'T FEEL PRESSURE TO DO THIS!

I know meeting in the week is tough with kids, work, etc. And if you can't come but want to just receive the emails, that is great too! If you do decide you want to do this, please just reply to this email and let me know. If I don't hear from you I promise I won't bug you with additional inbox material!

Our first meeting would be the on the first Wednesday of each month. My first email will go out on Monday and will follow every Monday after. If you have specific prayer requests, I want you to know this will be a safe place. You definitely don't have to share ANYTHING but if you want to, this will be confidential and I promise it will get prayed over.

Hoping you're having a great day and let me know if you're up for it when you get a chance. Again, no pressure!

Ashby

The response was overwhelmingly positive and the group kept growing in leaps and bounds without any sort of recruiting whatsoever. Honestly I wanted to keep it relatively small but it was having such a positive impact on the members that they were sharing with their friends and anyone who heard about it wanted in! We had women in eleven different states and three countries (including Japan and Germany) jumping on board. Quickly I realized that although the majority of the group would be done via email, the meetings were encouraging and important and that the group would benefit if there were more local chapters with smaller numbers.

Unsure of how to accomplish that, I started praying about the idea of somehow outlining what we did each month and providing email content so more groups could be easily formed. Shortly after, Estee (a group member) mentioned during one of our meetings how this group was really changing her marriage and she thought that the emails should be a book. Michelle (another member) chimed in saying she saved every email into a file on her computer. Kim and several other wives mentioned how they forwarded these emails on to other women and that they were too much of a help to marriages to *not* put into a book because so many others could benefit. Their vision lined up with a desire that was already growing in my heart.Thus this book was born: *The Warrior Wives Club*. With over three years of material at this point, I knew I could provide the emails for someone to have an entire year's worth of content to start their own group which would leave very little responsibility on the leader. And if they didn't want to start a group, the email content could serve as a weekly devotional and would bless someone's marriage just by reading it.

There have been so many marriages changed as a result of this group (mine included!) that it would feel selfish not sharing our experience (see testimonials at the end of the book!). In a little over three years, we have seen three marriages turn from divorce and get into biblical counseling. We've seen freedom from pornography addiction. We've kneeled and prayed with a woman who stood for her marriage despite his infidelity. We've seen another woman forgive her husband who is currently sober after years of drug addiction. We've seen intimacy restored in marriages after difficult and "cold" seasons. One woman gave her life to Christ and another started going to church with her family. The impact has been huge and the only explanation is prayer to an amazing God who loves and fights for marriages. Marriage is a tangible example of His covenant with us!

The theme of the *Warrior Wives Club* is to learn biblical truths to strengthen us to become "a wife of noble character" and to give us a safe community to fight for our marriages through the power of prayer. There is a war on marriage out there and being in battle alone isn't nearly as effective as standing shoulder to shoulder with others to lift each other up before God, especially when we no longer have the strength to go it alone. *The Warrior Wives Club* is not a gossip session or a place to husband bash. Rather, it's a safe place for you to share your heart and your prayers. What happens in WWC stays in WWC and respectful transparency can blossom within these boundaries.

If you want to see your marriage changed one week at time, I encourage you to read the exact emails and prayers that changed our marriages. If you want to see other marriages changed as well, start your own group! In part two of this book, you will find everything you need to do this whether you have a group of three women or thirty. By using this book as your resource to do most of the heavy lifting and asking God to lead you every step of the way, you will see an impact on your marriage and on the marriages of those you ask to come alongside you. A healthy, happy and holy marriage can influence many generations to come and change your life as you know it. For the better!

HOW TO USE THIS BOOK

In the following pages, you will find a weekly marriage devotional for any individual. If you choose to start your own group, these devotionals will serve as your first year of email content for your group and have been labeled as such. This book is complete with special challenges extended to each of your members during certain weeks, prayers to help transform your marriages and a section of insights written from different women within my group with wisdom they have learned from their own marriages.

Part two outlines the simple format for WWC: Weekly emails, monthly meetings and monthly prayer requests. The weekly emails are already written out for you and can be accessed in digital format by contacting me at ashbyduval@gmail.com. Then you simply need to copy and paste the week's content into your group weekly emails in addition to providing the next time you will meet and any monthly prayer requests. In this section emails and meetings are discussed in greater depth.

You will quickly find that all pertinent issues relating to marriage are addressed such as sex, personality differences, anxiety, finances, consequences of divorce, fighting fair, prioritizing marriage over your children instead of the other way around, and who the real Enemy of our marriages actually is. In addition, a consistent theme that is repeated throughout the weekly emails is to *pray it on them, don't lay it on them.*" One of the most refreshing things you will experience is that by being regularly reminded to refrain from criticizing or trying to change your husband, you will instead be praying and encouraging him. As a result, you will experience change in your own heart. What's interesting is that a heart change in our husbands often *follows* a heart change in ourselves. However, when our humility enables us to focus on their good, this change is a pleasant surprise rather than a burdensome expectation. True love is felt when there is freedom from judgement and people feel safe to be themselves.

Marriages are under attack. Two sinful people living in a fallen world already make marriage difficult and when Satan and our culture continually assault this beautiful covenant, this only adds to that difficulty. Our greatest weapon against the enemy as stated in **Ephesians 6:12-18 (NLT)** is prayer and the Word of God: **"For we are not fighting against flesh-and-blood enemies, but against evil rulers and authorities of the unseen world, against mighty powers in this dark world, and against evil spirits in the heavenly places. Therefore, put on every piece of God's armor so you will be able to resist the enemy in the time of evil. Then after the battle you will still be standing firm. Stand your ground, putting on the belt of truth and the body armor of God's righteousness. For shoes, put on the peace that comes from the Good News so that you will be fully prepared. In addition to all of these, hold up the shield of faith to stop the fiery arrows of the devil. Put on salvation as your helmet, and take the sword of the Spirit, which is the word of God. Pray in the Spirit at all times and on every occasion. Stay alert and be persistent in your prayers for all believers everywhere."**

Ephesians 6:14 says to "stand." This book will encourage you as you stand for your marriage with other women standing alongside of you, encouraging you and praying for you along the way. We are in a war and one of Satan's greatest weapons is to divide and conquer. When we are isolated, we are easier to destroy. By surrounding yourself with other warriors willing to fight for their marriage (and yours!), you will feel less alone and more equipped to face every season you will go through with your spouse. I'm excited to see what the Lord does in your marriage and other marriages through your heartfelt prayers as you arm yourself with scripture and stand arm in arm with other women with the greatest Warrior of all time leading the charge, Jesus Christ.

PART ONE
WEEKLY CONTENT AND PRAYERS

This section includes 52 weeks' worth of content you can use independently as a weekly devotional or that you can send out as an email if you choose to start your own group. The purpose is to remind you at the beginning of each week for an entire year to prioritize your marriage and pray for your spouse. Each email ends with a short prayer that you are encouraged to pray each day for the week so it can truly take root in your heart.

*Each devotional was written by Ashby Duval with the exception of the appendix. This special section has been written by other warrior wives within our group who generously shared their wisdom and marital experience in areas they could speak to in greater depth.

WEEK 1
WELCOME TO WARRIOR WIVES

Today marks the first day of our journey toward a better marriage! If you are reading this, you have expressed interest in joining the *Warrior Wives Club*. So, what is it? In a world where marriage is often mocked and attacked, it is important to take a stand against the enemy who seeks to destroy it. You may not be aware that you are in a spiritual war or that you even have an enemy but that is the absolute truth. John 10:10 says Satan comes to" kill, steal and destroy" and in 1 Peter 5:8 it says "Your adversary the devil prowls around like a roaring lion, seeking someone to devour." One of the primary things he wants to devour is marriage because it represents the covenant God made with us and its destruction leads to a downward cycle for generations to come. That's the bad news. But the good news is that in the same verse in John 10:10 it also says that Jesus came so that "you may have life and have it abundantly" and Jesus is stronger then Satan (1 John 4:4)! Your marriage is a covenant that must be fought for and defended at all costs. It is worth fighting for! But it's hard to do that on your own sometimes. First and foremost, our Savior Jesus is fighting with you and for you for your marriage to survive and thrive. The purpose of *Warrior Wives Club* is to give you weekly inspiration to remind you of that, to encourage you in your marriage and, should you choose to go through this book as a group, to receive the support and prayers of other women that are absolutely invaluable.

For the group format to work well, three simple rules need to be implemented:

RULE 1: What happens in *Warrior Wives Club* stays in *Warrior Wives Club*. Transparency is encouraged but only because it's a safe environment. You will be loved on and prayed for and you will not be exposed or gossiped about. What you share stays there. Accountability and community are a beautiful thing when people have a safe environment where they and their spouse are protected.

RULE 2: Never shame or uncover your husband. This is not a group where you can "husband bash." Speak with respect about him the way you would want him to speak about you.

RULE 3: Commit to not only praying for your spouse, but the other marriages as well when requests go out each month.

As we begin to fight the good fight, I want to remind you of the two weapons Ephesians 6 says we have: the word of God and prayer. These will be the focus of the weekly content. I'm so proud of you for starting this journey, whether on your own or with other women. The Lord loves the marriage covenant. It is the example He gave us to show us how He loves us no matter what! He will walk with you every step of the way and give you the strength to weather any storm you might face. You WILL be blessed by taking the time to invest in your marriage and this year of being intentional to pray for your spouse will yield results that will bless you for a lifetime.

Each week as you read each devotional, I encourage you to meditate on the topic throughout the course of the week and repeat the prayer so that you can truly grasp and apply each concept.

This first week is an excerpt from a book I HIGHLY recommend by Stormie Omartian called *The Power of the Praying Wife* which is listed in our resource section (in addition to several other books that will bless your marriage). You can get it from the library, Amazon or even download it on Kindle on your device. I actually have it on Kindle on my phone and it has really come in handy to have it right with me!

> "A wife's prayers for her husband have a far greater effect on him than anyone else's, even his mother's. (Sorry, Mom.) A mother's prayers for her child are certainly fervent. But when a man marries, he leaves his father and mother and becomes one with his wife (Matthew 19:5). They are a team, one unit, unified in spirit. The strength of a man and wife joined together in God's sight

is far greater than the sum of the strengths of each of the two individuals. That's because the Holy Spirit unites them and gives added power to their prayers. That's also why there is so much at stake if we don't pray. Can you imagine praying for the right side of your body and not the left? If the right side is not sustained and protected and it falls, it's going to bring down the left side with it. The same is true of you and your husband. If you pray for yourself and not him, you will never find the blessings and fulfillment you want. What happens to him happens to you and you can't get around it. This oneness gives us a power that the enemy doesn't like. That's why he devises ways to weaken it. He gives us whatever we will fall for, whether it be low self-esteem, pride, the need to be right, miscommunication, or the bowing to our own selfish desires. He will tell you lies like, "Nothing will ever change." "Your failures are irreparable." "There's no hope for reconciliation." "You'd be happier with someone else." He'll tell you whatever you will believe, because he knows if he can get you to believe it, there is no future for your marriage. If you believe enough lies, your heart will eventually be hardened against God's truth. In every broken marriage, there is at least one person whose heart is hard against God. When a heart becomes hard, there is no vision from God's perspective. When we're miserable in a marriage, we feel that anything will be an improvement over what we're experiencing. But we don't see the whole picture. We only see the way it is, not the way God wants it to become. When we pray, however, our hearts become soft toward God and we get a vision. We see there is hope. We have faith that He will restore all that has been devoured, destroyed, and eaten away from the marriage. 'I will restore to you the years that the swarming locust has eaten' (Joel 2:25). We can trust Him to take away the pain, hopelessness, hardness, and unforgiveness. We are able to envision His ability to resurrect love and life from the deadest of places."[1]

If you haven't ever prayed for your spouse on a regular basis, it's not too late! Prayer is the most powerful thing you can do for your marriage because of Who you are praying to: the God of the Universe. Jesus said in Matthew 19:26 "with man this is impossible, but with God all things are possible." No heart is too hard and no marriage is too hopeless for Him. We will start with short, small prayers but don't think for a moment your prayers for your spouse are small in our Father's ears. He is so proud of you for taking this covenant with Him seriously and will honor those prayers in huge ways.

Father God, thank You for giving us the gift of marriage. Thank You for giving us the gift of prayer, community, accountability and Your word to stand and fight for our marriages. I praise You that we are NEVER in this fight alone. You are with us and for us and if You are for us, who can be against us? (Romans 8:31) We love You Lord. We ask for Your protection and blessing over our marriages as we take this first step. Please bring to mind our spouses throughout the day so we may pray for them in the specific ways you press on our hearts. In the powerful name of Jesus Christ, Amen.

WEEK 2
WHEN OPPOSITES STOP BEING SO ATTRACTIVE

My husband has been moving his shop and showroom to a different location the last couple weeks. I am not quite a minimalist, but I hate clutter and I am constantly getting rid of things (sometimes before I should have!). So much so that I have been known to sneak things out of the house in the middle of the night to the garbage just so I won't get caught throwing away a giant stuffed penguin that no one should need. Ever. Only to be caught the next day because his stuffed head snuck its way out the top of the garbage can (traitor!).

Long story short, my spouse is not a minimalist. He needs #allthethings. His mindset is that someday he might need that one thing on a job site. This trait that used to be cute about him became irritating because I thought my way was better.

Isn't that the root of a lot of the fights couples have? Pride?

We think our way is better when sometimes it's not better or worse, just different. There is that age-old saying we've all heard, "opposites attract." At the beginning of our relationships, those things that made us so different were adorable, endearing, even charming. "Oh, isn't it cute how whimsical and scattered she is?" Or, "How wonderful that he is good with money and can save!" We were probably attracted to these qualities because they were different from what we were used to. Intrigued, if you will. But then we're a few years in and all of the sudden her messy closet is driving him nuts and his affinity towards savings means never spending money on anything unessential, which means her fun idea for a vacation gets squashed.

I totally believe that God purposefully put something in us to be attracted to different qualities so that we would make a good team. I'm not saying every marriage is made of exact opposites, but even the fact that we are male and female sets us up for a lot of differences!

Why is this? I think it goes back to the point Gary Thomas makes in his book, Sacred Marriage, that marriage is not supposed to make us happy.[1] Does it bring happiness? Sure! Is it a wonderful experience? At times, absolutely! But! It. Is. Hard! If you are in your marriage for the sole purpose of it bringing utter satisfaction and enjoyment, you will be hard-pressed to stay married. You will always be on the hunt for that elusive spouse who won't bring so much disturbance or conflict into your life.

To take it even further, what if these disturbances are part of the point of marriage? The things that are different than us and the things that rub us the wrong way or force us to think outside of our comfort zone challenge us and cause us to press into Jesus. Our spouse's sin is used to expose our own sin and vice versa. By entering into a covenant relationship where you have said that for better or for worse I'm going to stick this thing out, you are forced to love when you don't feel like loving, forced to forgive when you don't feel like forgiving, forced to come face-to-face with your own junk when all you want to do is think about his. The truth is, we are all messed up, which is why we all need Christ. Our sin is a reminder of that need. And oftentimes our "opposite" exposes that sin in our hearts. Sometimes it's the sin of being judgmental and self-righteous when we think they are in the wrong. Instead of showing them grace and praying for them, we are picking them apart. We start down that road of seeing all that is "wrong" and they become less "attractive" which is a very slippery slope.

Our challenge as their forever person, their one-flesh, is to catch those thoughts early and take them captive to obey Christ (2 Corinthians 10:5). We start by asking Him to take over, give us His mind, and help us see our spouse through His eyes. We also ask Him to expose our own sin and the motives of our hearts. This is a prayer He will answer. He is serious about marriage because He made marriage the outstanding symbol of His covenant with us. Ephesians 5:28-30 says, "In the same way, husbands ought to love their wives as they love their own bodies. For a man who loves his wife actually shows love for himself. No one hates his own body but feeds and cares for it, just as Christ cares for the church. And we are members of his body."

Let us be thankful for our opposites! Let us pray that during the times when they are being used to challenge us and open our eyes to our own sin that we would be grateful because God in His goodness and authority over all things appointed our opposites to make us more holy, more like Himself. To press us deeper into our relationship with Jesus. And if put in His hands, He can use our differences to press us deeper into our relationship with our spouse as well.

Father in Heaven, thank You for making us fearfully and wonderfully and hardwiring us to be attracted to things in our spouse that are the opposite of us. You created us to be a team with different strengths and weaknesses so that we could be a help to one another. I pray you would give us that perspective and give us new eyes to see and appreciate our husbands. We pray as we look to You that You would deepen our relationship with You first and then our spouse. We put our marriages in Your hands and pray You would protect them and mold them so we may bring You glory in them. It's in Jesus' powerful name that we pray, Amen.

WEEK 3
THE BLOT ON HIS SHIRT

On our way to a doctor's appointment for our third son's first check-up, Dominic and I were listening to an interview on Moody radio.[1] It covered a lot of different topics on marriage and the woman being interviewed was talking about Elisabeth Elliott which got my attention immediately because I LOVE HER. One of the things Elisabeth (Is it ok I use her first name? I feel like we will be best friends in heaven so I thought I'd get a jump start on our impending intimacy) said was to not focus on the "blot".

She said, if someone were wearing a perfect white shirt, no wrinkles, beautiful fabric, etc., but it had a pen stain on the pocket, we would disregard the rest of the shirt and notice only the ink blot. Having been widowed twice and now re-married once again, she said we have a tendency of doing the same thing with our husbands. We focus on the things that are wrong or that are "flawed" instead of focusing on all the amazing things about him. This jogged my memory about her book, *The Path of Loneliness*, where she said, "Having been married to three very different men, all of them fine Christians husbands, I have found that no one of them, or even all three of them together if I had even a polyandrist, could meet all my needs."[2] BECAUSE a person cannot possibly meet all your needs. You need Christ for that. Philippians 4:19 says, "And my God will supply every need of yours according to his riches in glory in Christ Jesus."

Only He can truly satisfy, and when we look to our husbands to complete us in a way only Jesus can, they will always fall short. We will tend to notice all the ways they fall short instead of enjoying them for one important aspect of who they were created to be in our lives: vessels of sanctification. Maybe not as romantic as what we had in our minds pre-marriage, but it is way more beautiful if you think about it. God picked this particular person to shape you and mold you more and more into His image and one of the ways marriage does that is by exposing our sin (oftentimes through the flaws of the other person!). When we recognize that Christ alone can satisfy, that frees us to see our marriages as opportunities to serve instead of focusing on how we can be served. With this mentality, there are a lot more opportunities for happiness instead of the disappointments we will inevitably face if we are always focused on their downfalls. When we celebrate someone's strengths and the good qualities they possess, we free them up to be the best version of themselves and the love between you will only multiply. There are a couple of people in my life where I feel like I disappoint them or that I have to prove myself to them. I find myself stressed and nervous around them and often end up behaving exactly like what I think THEY think I am like. It's exhausting!

On the contrary, there are some people in my life who literally think I can do no wrong. They often encourage me and point out my strengths and I find myself not only wanting to be around them as much as I can, but also I end up being an amazing version of myself. I feel free and safe to love and be loved and it's wonderful!

Here's a *Warrior Wives Club* challenge: Get your eyes off his blot! Figure out a way to remind yourself this week to focus on his good qualities and encourage him. Maybe wear a rubber band or bracelet? Maybe a little alarm on your phone to remind you once or twice a day? Maybe just write the word "blot" on your wrist with a big x through it? Just kidding. Sort of. Whatever works for you! Just take time to remember why you fell in love with him to begin with and actively look for the good in him. I strongly believe when we look for the bad we will find it and the same goes for the good. Cheers to a blot free week of loving your spouse well!

Father please help us take our eyes off of their blots. Thank You that our blots are covered and made white by the blood of Christ. We ask Your forgiveness for focusing too much on the things that are wrong instead of the beautiful, creative ways you made them. We pray we would allow You to do a deep work in our hearts by reminding us of the gospel and what Jesus did on that cross. In light of that, it makes it very difficult to focus on the wrongs of others. Please keep that fresh on our minds each day. It's in the name of Jesus Christ Himself we pray these things, Amen.

WEEK 4
THE POWER OF YOUR WORDS

Dominic and I were watching "Cinderella Man" with Russell Crowe and Renee Zelwegger the other night. It's an older movie about a boxer in the Great Depression trying to provide for his family.

There was a really touching part in the movie where all the bills were overdue and they were struggling with keeping the heat on in the dead of winter and unsure of how they would feed their three children. He looked at his wife with great defeat and sadness and told her how sorry he was. She looked back at him and smiled and said "No. No. No"[1] and climbed on his lap and kissed him. She was such a support to him, always had his back and the two were a genuine team in both life and parenting. I realized (although it was just a movie) that she had two choices there: Kick him while he was down by sharing her fears and frustrations or take the opportunity to remind him he was loved and she was proud of him and that they were in this together.

We often have the same choice. When they come home from the grocery store with the wrong items, when they parent a way that might be different than we would do it, when they don't manage their time well or do something unwise in our eyes...all opportunities. At the end of the day, our husbands don't want to fail us. They want our love and respect more than they could probably ever describe to us. Our words are so powerful. They can lift him up or tear him down and too often we tear down out of hurt, frustration, resentment, or exhaustion.

These verses in the book of Proverbs were very convicting to me:

"There is one whose rash words are like sword thrusts, but the tongue of the wise brings healing." Proverbs 12:18

"A soft answer turns away wrath, but a harsh word stirs up anger." Proverbs 15:1

"Gracious words are like a honeycomb, sweetness to the soul and health to the body." Proverbs 16:24

"Whoever restrains his words has knowledge, and he who has a cool spirit is a man of understanding." Proverbs 17:27

"A word fitly spoken is like apples of gold in a setting of silver." Proverbs 25:11

Women speak an average of 13,000 more words than men in any given day. I think because of that we have to be extra cautious of what is coming out of our mouths. I have often thought how much more gracious and thoughtful Dominic is with his words towards me than I am towards him. I tend to be the one to say something unnecessary or hurtful in the heat of the moment. I *want* to be a wife whose words edify and encourage him and that he would know by my tone and my tongue that he is loved, respected and that I am on his side. This doesn't mean I should never say something difficult to him or that we will never argue, but ideally I would love to listen more, speak less, and ask that the Holy Spirit would fill me with grace and love in the difficult and frustrating scenarios.

Sometimes being respectful means not saying something at all but just taking a bit of time to pray through it. Sometimes it's apologizing for saying something that was hurtful after the fact when we have those human (and let's face it...hormonal!) moments.

Last week I met with a young widower whose wife had past away from cancer four months ago. With tears in his eyes he said he felt like part of him had died. Boy did I remember that feeling all too well. The death of your spouse is like being ripped in half because technically as one flesh, you ARE. It reminded me of what a privilege it is to be "one flesh" and married and that what we speak over them, we are essentially speaking over ourselves as well. We don't know what our last words will be to anyone, and I certainly don't want mine to be nagging or unthoughtful. The night my first husband, Spencer, suddenly died, our last words were, "Love you, Baby." I can't imagine how much harder it would have been if they had been anything different.

The truth is, we will mess up and we ABSOLUTELY can't do this in our own strength, so below is a prayer for our sweet little group:

Father God, thank You for the gift of marriage, that it is a covenant that represents Your love for the church and for us individually. Thank You for the "one flesh" verses that remind us how serious this commitment is and that we are a part of one another in a way no other relationship will ever compare on this earth. Forgive us for using our words to hurt rather than heal and give us extra conviction to know when those times are, and conviction if there is something right now we need to ask forgiveness for. Give us grace to speak life over our husbands. Give us grace to hold our tongue when needed, to speak the hard words in love when needed, and to know how to encourage them in a way only we as their wives can. Will You give us insight this week into what they need? Will You give us YOUR eyes to see them and understand them? Will You speak to them and love them through us? We are Your precious daughters and willing vessels and we want to love well the sons You have given us to walk with through this life, and in a way that blesses them and pleases You. It's in Your powerful name Jesus that we pray these things. Amen.

WEEK 5
YOUR SPOUSE IS NOT
YOUR ENEMY

While visiting Spencer's family in Minnesota, I overheard my in-loves leading a group session in one of their "Married For Life" classes. They said to the couples, "Your spouse is NOT your enemy!" And repeated it. Then they made them repeat it! I giggled walking down the hall because it's so true! Sometimes the person who is supposed to be the closest to us in the world can feel like our enemy. And to be honest, our TRUE enemy (Satan) loves to stoke that fire. If he can divide us and convince us that our spouse is against us, he gets a foothold in our marriage. Divide and conquer. Isn't that a common war strategy?

In marriage, two people literally become one. They form a covenant that nothing and no one should break. If it does break, it does more than destroy a family. It also chips at our faith.

The only other covenant we have is with God Himself. He makes it with us and will *never ever ever* break it. Yet in our human nature, that seems too good to be true sometimes. We often think that if we do something bad enough or don't do enough good things, then He will be mad at us and maybe even stop loving us. No matter how many times scripture SCREAMS the opposite at us "Be strong and courageous. Do not fear or be in dread of them, for it is the LORD your God who goes with you. He will not leave you or forsake you." (Deuteronomy 31:6); "nor anything else in all creation, will be able to separate us from the love of God in Christ Jesus our Lord." (Romans 8:39) or the fact that Christ died on the cross for our sins so that we would be righteous in God's sight forever (nothing can make that untrue), we listen to that stupid devil who whispers to us "You're never going to be good enough. You have no hope. Hopefully you will get into heaven, but who knows after all the horrible stuff you've done."

Do you know my grandmother actually said that to me? She said if she didn't have a better attitude towards this person, she might not get into Heaven. She was listening to a lie of the enemy! If she knows Christ and believes He died for her and rose again, she can be as sure that she is going to Heaven as she is of her own name! When I had the privilege of replacing Satan's lie with the truth of the gospel and that she is completely forgiven, she grabbed my hands and kissed them as her tears fell in relief. It got me thinking…when the devil messes with the covenant of marriage, he messes with our faith, our kids' faith, and the faith of our family, friends and neighbors. Maybe not directly, but indirectly because if we are saying this person is "unforgivable," then there is a part of us that wonders if there is something in us that is unforgivable too. Our covenant in marriage is a representation of Christ's covenant with the church: unconditional love, forgiveness seventy times seven, grace upon grace and mercy upon mercy.

Our spouse is not our enemy. We have a very real enemy who wants us to believe that it's our spouse or someone or something else but don't be mistaken, *"For we are not fighting against flesh-and-blood enemies, but against evil rulers and authorities of the unseen world, against mighty powers in this dark world, and against evil spirits in the heavenly places"* (Ephesians 6:12 NLT). Next time you feel like you're in a war with your spouse, take a step back and realize that is not the reality. If he can keep us focused on a false enemy, he gets away with murder. Literally. Murder of our marriages. We have to recognize what is going on and pray accordingly.

You and (insert your husband's name here) are on the same team. He is not your enemy. You are one. Because of that oneness, our prayers for him are more powerful than they are for anyone else on this earth because you have an authority in that relationship more than any other, even your child's! You can fight for him and for your marriage in an unseen war every time you bow your head for your spouse. You. Are. Warriors. And when we pray with other warriors, we aren't in the trenches alone.

I realize some of you feel like you are on the front lines right now. You are taking some heavy hits and you might even feel as though you are fighting alone. I want to assure you that you are not. Hopefully you have other women right behind you and beside you praying (fighting) with you, but you *always* have your mighty and powerful Savior Jesus Christ out front taking the major hits. You are just experiencing some shrapnel. He is your shield (Psalm 28:7). He will fight for you. He IS fighting for you. And He is stronger than the enemy (1 John 4:4). Infinitely stronger. He has "Lord of Lords" tattooed on His thigh (Revelation 19:16) and He is the most passionate and powerful Warrior that has ever, or will ever, exist. He is not passive. He is not a wimp. He took time to make a whip out of rope and drove money changers out of a temple (John 2:15). He told the most prominent leaders in His day that they were vipers and sons of Satan (Matthew 12:34). He overcame death and He can overcome whatever you are facing. Give it to Him! Let Him fight your real enemy and fight *for* your marriage.

Father, we serve a MIGHTY God! Powerful, sovereign, protective, merciful and compassionate. You have already won this war. We know how this ends. But we pray we would not give any victories of the battles in this war to Satan. We know we can't fight him alone but You never asked us to. You asked us to stand. You said You would be our shield. You gave us brothers and sisters in Christ to pray and fight with us. We are not alone because You will never leave us or forsake us. In 1 Timothy 6:12 You tell us to fight the good fight of faith. May we do that with Your strength and grace. May we finish this race well. Please remind us with the conviction of Your Holy Spirit that our spouse is NOT our enemy. We have a real enemy but we need not be afraid. You word says in James 4:17 that if we submit to You and resist the devil, he will flee from us. So today, Lord, this moment, we bow and submit to You, resisting Satan's lies and going forward in truth as he runs from us. We are Your warrior princesses and we are on a mission for truth and for covenant. It's in THE Warrior's name, Jesus Christ, that we pray and ask these things. Amen.

WEEK 6
WEED YOUR OWN GARDEN

A wise friend once told me that before you get married, ask all the couples in your life whom you respect and have a marriage worth emulating what their best advice to you would be.

Thinking this was quite brilliant, I spent the months leading up to my wedding doing just that. Some of the advice I loved most were to prefer your spouse to everyone else in your actions and decisions, to make a conscious effort to look for the good in your spouse, to avoid "keeping score" but focus on serving instead and last but not least to "weed your own garden." This last one is what inspired the *Warrior Wives Club*.

One of the biggest mistakes you can make in your marriage is to constantly focus on what is wrong with your spouse, on their weaknesses, failures, character flaws, and mistakes. Since you have enough weeds in your own garden to keep you busy for a lifetime, you should focus on the areas you need to work on and stop wasting energy on what you *think* your spouse needs to change.

Simple enough, right? Wrong! I discovered it was quite easy to point out the negative in my spouse while naively thinking I was just delightful and smelling of roses and lavender. But the truth is, we all have things that are wrong with us. However, there is only one person in this world that you can change (hint: it's not your spouse!). Case in point: when we got married, my husband loved smoking cigars. When we first met I thought it was kind of cool and sexy, maybe even endearing, until I realized that this was actually a big addiction and fueled my fear of him dying. It was making me a crazy person. Literally! I pleaded, cried, tried guilting him, etc., but nothing worked! It just drove a huge wedge between us.

Going back to that precious advice, I decided to "pray it on him, not lay it on him." (My mother in law's words, not mine.) I simply quit bringing up this touchy subject. He knew he needed to quit; he *obviously* knew how I felt about it since I never missed an opportunity to tell him. Since my elaborate and dramatic speeches got me nowhere, I was actually going to apply those words and "weed my own garden." I started by reading the book *One Day at Time in Al-Anon.* The book's main premise is to help you realize you do not have the power to change someone, you cannot control someone and therefore you cannot let their actions control you either. They have great sayings like "live and let live" and "let go and let God."[1] It put me in a great mindset and encouraged me to pray and ask God to work on *my* shortcomings.

Weeding my own garden did two things:
1. It gave me the humility to see that I had enough junk in my own life that I didn't need to point out anyone else's.
2. It reminded me that I'm not in control over anyone nor can I change anyone—which gave me so much freedom! (And I'm sure him too!)

About six months after I started applying this great truth, my husband came to me and told me he had quit smoking. After I picked my jaw up off the floor and did a happy dance to the internal song playing in my head, "Whoomp! There It Is," I composed myself long enough to ask him, "For how long?" He told me going on three weeks.

He also shared that when I quit bringing it up and he didn't feel like he had to hide it from me anymore, his focus switched from guilt and shame and secrecy to a genuine conviction and determination to stop. He didn't say this, but I realized I had actually been an obstacle to him quitting. When I got out of the way, he was able to take his eyes off the distracting, insane lady waving her arms and crying and stomping like a toddler to actually see the problem clearly.

Marriage is hard even in the best of circumstances. You have two very flawed people coming together in a situation where those flaws have nowhere to hide. You are completely exposed for probably the first time in your life! There is a great point from Gary Thomas in his book, *Sacred Marriage,* that basically says most of the time people don't leave their marriage because of their spouse's sin, but because of their own.[2] It's hard to be confronted with all the things that are wrong with us, which is why I think it's easier for us to point at our spouse's flaws rather than have the courage to deal with our own.

What we don't understand is that there is so much beauty in looking for the good in someone instead of the bad. When we take the time to genuinely look at ourselves and what would make us a better person and spouse, we are able to remain humble and empathetic towards others. Freedom from judgement and negativity is absolutely incredible for not only you, but those around you. So whether it's your spouse or some other relationship you are struggling in, get out those gardening gloves, look up and in instead of out, and start yanking! You will be better for it and so will your marriage.

Father God, You knit us together in our mother's womb. YOU did that. You don't make mistakes. Help us remember that when we look at our spouse. Help us remember that because You created them, You will work on them in Your way, in Your own timing just like You are working on us. I pray we would allow You to pull up the weeds in your own garden and that our soil would be soft and easy to work with. We want to honor You with our lives and we know You love us so much… too much to leave us the way we are. We submit to Your loving hand as You remove the things in our lives that don't bring You glory and leave us in bondage. It's in the name of Jesus who died to set us free that we ask these things. Amen.

WEEK 7
DISAPPOINTED IN YOUR MARRIAGE?

Did you know that men primarily struggle with being selfish within their marriage while women primarily struggle with feeling disappointed? In the DVD that accompanies the book *Sacred Marriage*, Gary Thomas gave the example that if he asks an engaged woman about her fiancé, she will go on and on about how wonderful he is. If he asks a married woman about her husband however, he often gets a list of the things he is NOT. In prayer one night, he asked the Lord, "When does that shift happen?" It happens within marriage because we have preconceived notions of how marriage is supposed to be, and what kind of husband, man and father we thought they would be. Often they fall short of how we have them built up in our minds.

It was a great exercise to think about. If someone asked you right now about your husband, what would you say? He made the point to say, "If God's design for marriage is to teach how to love and be less selfish, you can see how our desires and God's desires might conflict. Until we align ourselves with God's purpose for marriage, we may not only resent our spouse, we might ultimately resent marriage itself because it seems designed to put us in situations where our selfishness is confronted. If marriage is about learning to love, it's about learning to walk out the biblical mandate to grow in love."[1]

Growing in love is often tested with these "disappointments" and high expectations. We are human and so are they. We have flaws and so do they. It's just easier to see theirs sometimes! I would love to challenge you to look for the good in your spouse this week. Thomas left us with the prayer to start our day with: "Lord, how do I love my spouse today like they've never been loved before and never will be loved again?"[2]

When we look at our marriages as an opportunity to serve and to love, we really begin to enjoy our spouses again. We had some great discussion last week about some tangible ways we could serve our spouses. Here are a few ideas we came up with:

First, pray the Lord would give you insight into his needs and how you could serve and love him in a way that would mean a lot to him.

Maybe make his favorite appetizer or dinner as a surprise.

Offer to give him a massage.

If you notice he's been really stressed or tired, give him an opportunity to rest.

Instead of having a to-do list waiting for him on the evenings or weekends, ask him what he would like to do.

Speak love over him. Encourage him in the areas you love about him or see that he is really trying or excelling in.

Jesus came not to be served but to serve (Matthew 20:28). Lord, may we serve our husbands as if serving You because that is the example You gave to us! Thank You for coming to this Earth and enduring all that You did to show us how important this is. Please help us love and serve them with Your love and by Your grace. We know in our flesh our proclivity is to be critical and complaining, making notes of our unmet expectations. Lord, I pray we would lay our expectations at Your feet. I pray You would give us eyes to see the good and words to speak that good out. We need You and love You, Lord. In the powerful name of Jesus we pray. Amen.

WEEK 8
ALL IS NOT LOST

I know I've said this several times before but one of the reasons I have content for emails each week is because I can be a total mess! God uses my sin and the lessons He's teaching me, and thankfully my sweet husband is OK with using our own examples because if it helps one other person, then it's worth it!

Saturday night Dominic and I had a doozy of a fight. We don't fight very much and honestly, both of us aren't even sure how this escalated so quickly but looking back, I think it was miscommunication on both our parts. I wasn't understanding where he was coming from and he wasn't understanding where I was coming from and as a result, there were heated and hurtful words exchanged.

Normally, this would have kept me awake all night. But when I realized we needed a minute and that our exchange wasn't getting us anywhere good, I retreated to our bedroom and opened up the *Armor of God* Bible study I'm doing written by Priscilla Shirer. Ok. That wasn't exactly the *first* thing I did. The first thing I did was cry and feel sorry for myself and think *crazy* things like "Fine! I won't say a single word to him tomorrow! Let him just think about all this!" And, "Jerk!! If he wants to be like that I'll just do my thing and he can do his thing and we can just co-habitate!" God convicted me pretty quickly that Satan was involved in this fight and that those thoughts weren't thoughts of Him. These are not the kind of things Jesus would say to do. So when I prayed, I asked Him to give me His thoughts and not to let Satan have one inch in our marriage. My very next thought was, "If you're identity is in Me, you don't need to be right or prove your point. If your identity is in Me, you can forgive quickly and even more, you need to ask forgiveness regardless if he does the same. If your identity is in Me, you can love him unconditionally and see him clearly through My eyes."

Well, OK then. Identity. My identity *is* in Christ but my feelings were still hurt. What do I do with that? I kept repeating the truth of scripture until my feelings lined up with what is true.

"I have been crucified with Christ. It is no longer I who live, but Christ who lives in me. And the life I now live in the flesh I live by faith in the Son of God, who loved me and gave himself for me." (Galatians 2:20).

"Make allowance for each other's faults, and forgive anyone who offends you. Remember, the Lord forgave you, so you must forgive others." (Colossians 3:13 NLT).

"For we do not wrestle against flesh and blood, but against the rulers, against the authorities, against the cosmic powers over this present darkness, against the spiritual forces of evil in the heavenly places. (Ephesians 6:12).

"This is my commandment, that you love one another as I have loved you." (John 15:12).

Next I wrote out a prayer and literally confessed all this truth. I said that God was bigger than our fight, *any* fight, and that what Satan meant for harm, the Lord could use for good (Genesis 50:20). Then I asked Him what my part in it was and asked Him to show me the ways I had hurt Dom. Shoot. That was a tough prayer to have answered. I was so self-righteous thinking I was justified in my anger when the Lord showed me with excruciating clarity that something I had said was like a knife in my husband's heart. I immediately asked His forgiveness and the next morning that was the first thing I did to Dom, asked his forgiveness and was specific about why. What could have turned into a whole weekend event if left up to me turned out to be quick, revealing, and even helpful, because what I'm realizing is that God can actually *reverse* Satan's schemes. Oftentimes I think something is ruined forever. That we won't ever come back from this or that, but that is a LIE. There is nothing God can't use for good for those who love Him if placed in His hands (Romans 8:28).

Are you believing the lie that things are too far gone and you can't come back from it? Stop! It's not true! Our actions flow out of what we believe. That's why it's *imperative* to stay in the Word of God. I mentioned earlier the *Armor of God* study (I can't recommend it enough by the way!! So amazing!) and the verse I read today said, "All things become visible when they are exposed by the light, for everything that becomes visible is light..." (Ephesians 5:13). Priscilla Shirer made the point that we often make decisions based on feelings, past experiences, instinct or intellect...all of which can change. She says, "I'm not suggesting that feelings, intellect and instinct can never help you in making life decisions. I'm simply saying that ultimately nothing should be trusted to govern your life like an unchangeable standard."[1] The one thing that doesn't change is the Word of God and it's light exposes the dark for what it is. We have a real enemy who wants to deceive us, divide our relationships, discourage us, place distrust in us towards God, and distract us. But as Corrie Ten Boom says, "Here I was weak and sinful, and there was the Devil, much stronger than me. But there was Jesus, much much stronger than the Devil. And together with Him, I was more than a conqueror."[2]

Romans 8:31-39 says:

> "What then shall we say to these things? If God is for us, who can be against us? He who did not spare his own Son but gave Him up for us all, how will He not also with Him graciously give us all things? Who shall bring any charge against God's elect? It is God who justifies. Who is to condemn? Christ Jesus is the one who died—more than that, who was raised— who is at the right hand of God, who indeed is interceding for us. Who shall separate us from the love of Christ? Shall tribulation, or distress, or persecution, or famine, or nakedness, or danger, or sword? As it is written,'For your sake we are being killed all the day long; we are regarded as sheep to be slaughtered.' No, in all these things we are more than conquerors through Him who loved us. For I am sure that neither death nor life, nor angels nor rulers, nor things present nor things to come, nor powers, nor height

nor depth, nor anything else in all creation, will be able to separate us from the love of God in Christ Jesus our Lord."

Your take away today (or at least my take away from this whole event) is:

Don't trust your feelings. They can be deceitful.

Pray for clarity and stay in the Word of God to see the truth.

Repent and ask for forgiveness quickly. Don't sit on it, which gives Satan room to wreak havoc. Then thank God for His forgiveness so Satan can't accuse you later.

Nothing is ruined if placed in God's hands. No matter how hopeless or hurt you are feeling. Jesus can reverse and even bring good out of it.

You are more than a conqueror through Him who loves us.

Heavenly Father, I pray You would expose any lies we are believing. I pray like Your Word says in 2 Corinthians 10:4 that we use Your mighty weapons to knock down the strongholds of human reasoning and destroy false arguments, and that we would destroy every proud obstacle and capture our rebellious thoughts and teach them to obey Christ. I pray that each woman in this group would be encouraged that although Satan is strong, and definitely after their marriage, that YOU are much stronger and FOR their marriage. His power is limited where YOUR power is unlimited. I pray we would have a hunger for Your Word, Your truth like never before and that we wouldn't just read it, but act on it by the power of Your Spirit. I pray we would keep short accounts with You and with our spouses, quickly asking forgiveness. I pray for protection over each of these women and their precious covenants. We love You, Lord, and can do nothing apart from You, so I pray we wouldn't even try but would start each of our days surrendered to You, empty vessels for You to fill us with Your Spirit. In the powerful name of Jesus I pray, Amen.

WEEK 9
LET HIM HELP YOU

Do you ask your husband for help? Do you get mad when he doesn't? Do you make it too hard on him with high expectations? One week we were all really sick and I told Trooper he needed a bath and Dominic offered to give it to him. I told him that was sweet and thank you but that I wanted to steam the room first with Eucalyptus oil to relieve congestion and put ginger root in the bath to help with his cough. He laughed. I asked him why and with a playful smile he said, "I don't know what I was thinking that this could be simple. You know honey, a lesser man would quit asking to help but I want you to know that I'm not going to do that."

Then I asked him what he meant and he said that oftentimes when he wants to help, I don't let him and he thinks it's because I have a certain way of doing things that is more complicated than he would make it. And to take it even further, he also thinks it will eventually cause tension in our marriage because I could start resenting him at some point for not helping. I honestly didn't know how to respond and prayed about it that night quite a bit. Here is what God put on my heart for me personally, although for you it could obviously be different:

One, I didn't want to totally depend on him, because of my fear of him dying. Yikes. So in essence, I've been one foot in, one foot out in this marriage out of fear and post traumatic stress from my first husband's sudden death. When Spencer died, one of the hardest things was having to re-learn how to do all the things I had come to depend on him for. Now with Dominic, I've been trying to do it all myself in case that ever happened again. Double Yikes.

Two, I was trying to earn love. This has been a hard walk for me in the faith department for years as it is the opposite way that God loves us. His agape love is totally unconditional. The One who made us and knows us the most lavishly loves us the most, *despite* all of our sin. There is nothing we can do to earn His love or lose it. With Dom (and pretty much all my relationships), I have a tendency towards trying to earn love at one point or another. I want to prove to them that I'm lovable and worth keeping around. This sounds crazy even as I type it but it's just so like the Lord to show us the deep, dark places in our hearts we don't even know are there. So when I make Dom a lunch to take to work, or don't ask him to take out the trash out to try and earn his favor, my motives are all wrong. If I make him a lunch because I love him and want to make his day easier, good! But I need to start questioning why I'm doing things...not just with him but with a-lot of people-pleasing things I tend to say yes to with the wrong motives. "For am I now seeking the approval of man, or of God? Or am I trying to please man? If I were still trying to please man, I would not be a servant of Christ" (Galatians 1:10).

After having a good cry and asking for help, God continued His lesson with me in a couple different ways. One was a Beth Moore Bible study I've been doing called *The Patriarchs*. One of her lessons gave the example of how for years she would be frustrated that her husband, Keith, was perfectly content doing "nothing" on the couch when she got home and had a million things that still needed to be done and how frustrated she would get. On one such day, out of pure frustration she asked if he would help her get dinner started. He jumped up and said, "Baby, I'd do anything for you. What do you need?" She stood there in awe and thought, *That's it? All I had to do was ask?*[1] Which leads me to another possible cause that could be a lack of communicating how specifically we would like their help. One friend mentioned that control was often her root issue. She thought it was just easier to do it herself since she knew she would have to go into detail to explain it to her husband in order for him to do it "correctly".

Often we can start resenting our husbands for not seeing the ways we need help and rather than asking him, we just continue on until we become bitter or we stunt him by criticizing or not allowing him to help just because it might be different than what we would do. We forget that God created us differently for a reason and that instead of focusing on our differences, we should celebrate them. Maybe there is a simpler way to do something. Or maybe if they do it differently, it might not be the end of the world like we sometimes think.

And sometimes, if your husband is anything like mine, he might just be too stressed or overworked to even see that you might be drowning yourself! This might be a time where we have to show them grace and take on more. In that situation, pray for wisdom on how to not let it get to the point of resentment, or total self-sufficiency, which can lead to separate lives instead of the one-flesh mentality God meant for marriage.

Women are complicated and capable creatures. We are able to do so many things at once and our capability can often lead to a freezing out of our spouse and might I even say, God? How often we try and do things in our own strength when we could be asking the Almighty Maker of Heaven and Earth who has endless resources and never gets stressed or has too much on His plate to help us! Our culture glorifies busyness and independence but our God WANTS us to depend on Him. I believe our husbands want to be dependable as well and sometimes we don't give them that opportunity.

Lord, we pray we could become more dependent on You in every way. It's in that dependence where true freedom begins. It's so exhausting trying to do everything in our strength and it's not what You want for us. There are dinners to make, laundry to be done, a never ending "TO DO" list and we feel overwhelmed. We want to be good helpmates to our husbands, but we want to have the right motives and allow them to bless and help us as well. We don't want to go down different paths doing our own thing. Lord, unite each of these women with their husbands in a way they have never been united before. Give us a "one flesh" mentality so we can do life together, bless and encourage each other, help one another and mainly glorify You with our marriage. We can't do it on our own. We are so grateful You never get tired of hearing our prayers. We are so grateful you have endless resources and are able to do more than we ever imagined. Please, Lord, do more than we ever imagined in our marriages. Help us as women to pray for each other and our spouses, spur one another on towards good works and encouraging words and in the meantime, grow closer to You than ever before. We need You. We love You. We surrender to You. In your powerful name, Jesus, we pray these things. Amen.

WEEK 10
DO HIM GOOD

I heard the most amazing sermon called "Queen of Your Husband's Heart" by Jill Briscoe. It's part of a series called *Queen of Hearts* that I got on CD from one of her speaking engagements and but you can also find it here: http://www.oneplace.com/ministries/ telling-the-truth-for-women/listen/queen-of-your-husbands-heart-458677.html

Without giving away too much before you have a chance to listen, I just have to share a verse she spoke about in Proverbs 31:12: "She does him good, and not harm, all the days of her life."

The verse isn't talking about "making him good" which can result in us trying to change them (which we are incapable of) and results in their unhappiness. The verse refers to "doing them good" which is consciously thinking of ways to bless them and bring happiness into their lives.

God has been teaching me this exact concept over the last few months, namely in praying for my husband about things that are issues before ever bringing them up. There are so many ways this has resulted in blessings but I wanted to give you a personal example.

Dominic loves what he does. Even when he's not working, he is most often building *something*, even if it's just legos with our oldest son Trooper. Before he met me, he spent all of his time either working on his business or building a youth camp. He never took a day off and would work late into the night. One of the things I absolutely love about him is that he is very present wherever he is. If he's with us, he is truly focused on us. However, the flip side is if he's at work, he's really there and it's hard for him to pull away at a decent time because he usually doesn't even know what time it actually is! I asked repeatedly for him to call to tell me if he's going to be running late and he would for about a week, and then he'd start forgetting again. We tried a calendar alarm but same thing, about a week in we were back to normal. I think we spent the first year in constant turmoil over this. Nagging him and guilting him sure weren't working (do they ever?). I finally realized I didn't have the power to change him and God is the only one who can. We had both been single for four years prior to meeting each other and it would take time for this team to form and I needed to trust that God was working on both of us to become a "we." He showed me some ways I wasn't being a team player either in regards to finances and parenting.

So, over the next couple of months, anytime I would get annoyed about this, I would just pray. I thanked God that he was a hard worker but prayed for him to find balance and just left it in God's hands. I would put his dinner on a nice plate where he could easily heat it up when he got home and focused on ways I could "do him good." You know what happened? God changed *my* heart in the process. He helped me see this wasn't Dom hurting me but it was a genuine habit that had formed over the years. Tenderness replaced my anger as I saw it would take time and that I had plenty of my own things to work on. It really changed my countenance towards him and increased how we trusted each other when there wasn't constant complaining. There weren't conditions for acceptance or love but a genuine feeling of being on the same side in this and praying together to become a team. He ended up being more open with me about how he was stressed about work and that going from being a single guy to a husband and dad of two almost overnight was overwhelming. He felt the intense pressure to provide and didn't want to fail at that. Yikes. Talk about eating humble pie! I hadn't even thought of how that might feel.

Somewhere along the way, it became common for him to be home for dinner more than not. And if he is running late, he almost always texts or calls. When he forgets he genuinely apologizes and I quickly and genuinely forgive knowing that it wasn't intentional. By focusing on not trying to change him but do him good, it created an atmosphere of trust and love that was unconditional. My mother-in-law always says, "Don't be Holy

Spirit Junior. Let God work on you and you pray for him." Isn't that the truth? I'm going to leave you with a little prayer about this and also an encouragement to listen to that link above. It really will bless your marriage in so many ways!

Heavenly Father,
Thank You that You love us with an unconditional love. Thank You that we don't have to stop or start anything for You to love us any more or any less but that when You look at us, You're absolutely crazy about us. You see us as righteous and lovely, and the parts that need work, You lovingly and tenderly attend to in Your perfect timing. Thank You that we can't change anyone because if we could, we would be controlling and prideful. Thank You that in surrendering to You and depending on You for help there is true freedom. Thank You that we have the freedom to love our husbands with Your unconditional, agape love and that we can do them good all the days of their lives because their lives are in Your hands and they are much safer in Yours than ours.

Lord, help us "pray it on them and not lay it on them." That is never an easy thing to do.We are dependent on You to remind us to do it and give us the grace and strength to trust You with our spouses and the things they need help with. We place our marriages in Your hands. We want to have marriages that honor You and encourage others who are looking in. We want them to see that there is something different about our marriages and families and that that difference is You at the center of everything we are and do. Mold us, Jesus. We are clay in Your loving hands and we trust You. Please give us specific insight this week into how to love our husbands and do good to them in a way that blesses them and encourages them. We love You so much, Lord. We are so thankful we are not in this alone. You are able to do anything and everything and You have given us amazing women to walk through this part of our journey together with as an added bonus. Your generosity and kindness blow us away. It's in Your powerful name, Jesus, that we praise You, thank You and ask these things, Amen.

WEEK 11
LONELINESS IN YOUR MARRIAGE

Have you ever experienced loneliness in your marriage? When I was pregnant with Trooper I was really sick. My first husband Spencer was a lot of amazing things but empathy was not his gift. In fact when he went to Haiti on a mission trip, he told me some people sarcastically nicknamed him "Mr. Compassionate". Ha! Long story short, he thought I was being a tad dramatic since my nausea never resulted in actual puking and my endless headaches, fatigue and feelings of being carsick put a strain on us. I was married, but felt alone. Thankfully it was only for a short season but I'll never forget that feeling.

I brought this topic up to Dom the other night and asked if he ever felt alone. He said no and asked if I did to which he answered before I could: "You do, don't you. At least sometimes?" He's pretty intuitive because he knows that sometimes I do. It's usually only for a few days during a busy work week for him and we are able to reconnect on the weekends but I'd venture to say that most (if not all) marriages might have a season that could vary from a few days to potentially weeks, months or years depending on the circumstances. This might be a tender area for some if this is a season you're currently in but my encouragement to you is this: it can be redeemed. God uses loneliness in the most beautiful ways. One of my favorite books of all time is called *The Path of Loneliness* by Elisabeth Elliott. Kate jokingly called it my "Don't Jump" book because I read that thing over and over following Spencer's death. I still can't look at the title without hearing her joke and cracking a smile!

One of my favorite quotes from the book says, "Loneliness comes over us sometimes as a sudden tide. It is one of the terms of our humanness, and, in a sense, therefore, incurable. I have found peace in my loneliest times not only through acceptance of the situation, but through making it an offering to God, who can transfigure it into something for the good of others."[1]

In our lonely times, God often speaks to us because He has our attention ("Therefore, behold, I will allure her, and bring her into the wilderness, and speak tenderly to her." Hosea 2:14). In seasons of loneliness you have nowhere else to turn. And in recognizing there is little to do but wait it out, we can turn that time into an incredible worship opportunity. By bringing the Lord our hurts, our pain and our loneliness, He can do so much more with it than if we held onto it. He can actually do amazing things and make your marriage stronger than ever. The thing is, our husbands are not and cannot be our everything. Just like we can't be theirs. Only Christ can handle that title because His shoulders are big enough to bear such pressure and His character is the only one capable of that kind of faithfulness.

We can and should enjoy our precious spouses and pray for extended periods of oneness and deep connection. But due to our humanness, there will undoubtedly be times of loneliness. I hope you don't feel that way right now but pray that if or when you do, you will bring it to the Lord's feet and lay it there as an act of worship. And that you would patiently watch as He lovingly brings something beautiful out of it. Isaiah 40:31 says "but they who wait for the LORD shall renew their strength; they shall mount up with wings like eagles; they shall run and not be weary; they shall walk and not faint." He will remind you that you are never truly alone and that He is never going anywhere and will always be with you. In this crazy world, that assurance means everything.

Lord, I pray for the current lonely hearts and the future ones. I pray we would entrust those times to You and ask for Your grace to endure them as we wait for You to reconnect us to our husbands once again. We know that we can do all things through Christ who gives us strength according to Your word so we pray for the strength to be content and bind our wandering hearts to You. May our entire lives be an act of worship, especially the lonely times so that we may draw closer to You in an unprecedented way. In Jesus' name we pray, Amen.

WEEK 12
THE SNARE TO COMPARE

I'm sure we've all heard of the danger of comparing ourselves to other people. It can rob us of our joy and undermine the thoughtfulness and love that the Lord had when making you in such a fearful and wonderful way. I wonder, can the same danger come from comparing our marriages to another? If we are both fearfully and wonderfully made, completely differently from anyone else on the planet and so is our spouse, wouldn't that make our marriages completely unique as well?

When I first married Spencer, I completely idolized his parents' marriage. They have been married over 40 years and are still very much in love. I had never seen that before at that point in my life so I thought in order for my marriage to look like that, I needed to do everything they did. They work together and have only couple friends and you will very rarely see them apart.

When I tried to do that in my marriage with Dominic, it was completely unrealistic. I don't know how to remodel a kitchen, bathroom or garage and even if I could, I'm still not going to go on a job site with him with four young children. Does this mean our marriage won't last? Of course not! It means I married a unique and wonderful man and if laid at the Lord's feet, our marriage will look exactly as He means for it to look.

We can make the same mistake when comparing our marriages that we can when comparing ourselves to others. 2 Corinthians 10:12 says "Not that we dare to classify or compare ourselves with some of those who are commending themselves. But when they measure themselves by one another and compare themselves with one another, they are without understanding." If we think someone else has a better marriage, it will rob us of our joy and we will try and emulate it in frustration since we are not the same people with the same backgrounds or the same circumstances. On the flip side, we can get caught up in judging other marriages thinking "They are really messed up!" Yet with this mindset, there is no way we can know exactly what they are going through or what the Lord might be doing. This only leaves us in place of judgment and condemnation which is both sinful and harmful. "For with the judgment you pronounce you will be judged, and with the measure you use it will be measured to you." Matthew 7:2.

The next time you are tempted to compare yourself to that "perfect" marriage you see on TV or social media, stop and remind yourself that your marriage is unique and beautiful in it's own way because the Lord has created each of you uniquely and beautifully *before* you were one flesh. And now that you are one flesh, that beauty most certainly did not go away but is growing each day you stay in your marriage and submit it to the leadership of Christ.

And the next time you are tempted to think yourself better than the marriage next door, remember they might be in a difficult season and that you are not immune to difficult seasons either.

Thank You, God, for whatever season we are in. If we place our marriage safely in Your hands, then it is exactly where it's supposed to be. If it's difficult now, we pray we will weather the storm by Your grace alone and if it's a particularly calm time, we praise You and pray we would appreciate it. You are our shield of love. We hide behind You. In Christ's name, Amen.

WEEK 13
BUSYNESS — BADGE OF HONOR OR SEAL OF DEATH?

As much as I look forward to the autumn season after a laid back summer (especially #allthingspumpkin), I often find myself totally overwhelmed and burned out by October. This year, I really felt God preparing my heart for a different approach. Specifically, He was emphasizing that the peace of our home is often up to me as a wife and mother. My mood can literally dictate the ambience of our sanctuary. Things that can assault your peaceful ambience can sneak in, *especially* this time of year. Our culture promotes busyness like it's a badge of honor, something to be proud of and that if you aren't signed up for a hundred different things that there is something wrong with you. Social media definitely perpetuates this because we are shown all the highlight reels but none of the chaos or stress that ensues between each glorious picture.

Let me tell you something that I'm noticing: this is killing marriages and families. Literally. I sound dramatic but it's true! Families are so busy shuffling here and there, being involved in this hobby or that commitment that the idea of a family dinner or actual conversation is falling to the waste side. Quality time is the thing that happens as a result of quantity time. It can't be planned out or scheduled in and those important connections that happen as a result of quality time are becoming casualties to our over-scheduled, overtired lives. Our relationships (the only thing that count for anything in the eternal) are suffering due to the distractions that scream for our attention and our own addiction to productivity, self-focus and instant gratification. Fear of missing out, seeking the approval of others, trying to find your identity in something or someone other than Christ, pursuits of fleeting happiness and a focus on the temporal instead of the eternal are all roots to this dilemma. Colossians 3:2 says "Set your minds on things that are above, not on things that are on earth." Busyness is the exact enemy of this scripture because we are too focused on the things that won't really matter in long-term.

The Lord convicted me a couple of months ago that no one is looking at my to-do list but me. No one knows if I get everything done on it or not and that these things that I make life or death in my head are nothing of the sort. The anxiety and feelings of being overwhelmed were completely self-induced. This became even more evident when I became pregnant with our fourth child and was super sick all the time. Panic set in because just to get through a normal day took everything I had. Simple tasks like going to the grocery, making meals and trying to homeschool made me want to cry. However, what I discovered in that process was both humbling and freeing. My kids were thrilled to have me be still on the couch for them to snuggle with or read to. Peanut butter sandwiches and smoothies sustained them just fine. My oldest was still learning and growing in school and all the things on my "important list" were still waiting for me a couple months later and no one died. Turns out I'm not nearly as important as I think I am. Ha! What a relief! Like Martha in the Bible, Jesus was inviting me to sit at His feet like Mary which is the better thing. I needed to get back to basics. Get back to delighting in Him and loving and serving my family with His grace and strength. I read something from a wonderful book called *Teaching from a Place of Rest* that said "if there is anything that is robbing you of peace, it needs to be cut out."[1] Peace needs to be a pre-requisite of your home, not an option. There is a commercial on Moody Radio that says that chaos is Satan's signature and that peace is Jesus' signature. Is chaos, stress, tension and feelings of being overwhelmed the undertone of your home right now or is it peace, love and joy? If it's the former and not the latter, it's time to sit down and answer a tough question: What. Needs. To. GO! Your list of accomplishments and achievements are not worth risking your marriage for. Seemingly innocent things, even "good" things aren't good if they take you away from what the Lord has entrusted to you.

The past few months I began saying no to things. I didn't even give excuses. If it was going to put me in a tizzy, take me away from my spouse or children too often, or put any of us under unnecessary stress, the answer was no. It's been so liberating! And guess what! No one really noticed! Except us and it was a delightful change. My husband Dominic said that when he drove away the other morning, he smiled because our home was full of peace and his kids and wife were full of smiles. It set the tone for his day. This filled me with such gratitude for what the Lord had put on my heart and the ways He had done it! First with the to-do list, then with a daily reminder of Colossians 3 for weeks about focusing on the eternal and not the temporary, followed by our pregnancy and the limitations it forced on me. These very limitations ended up leading to the discovery of some very real freedoms. Isn't that just like the Lord?

One last thing: Jordan from our group posted on her instagram page that we are human BE-ings not DO-ings. My challenge to you this season is to BE still before God (Psalm 46:10). Ask Him to prioritize the things in your life that need to stay and highlight the things that need to go. It's in the stillness where He talks to us. It's in the margin we have in our lives that gives room for the Lord to move and work on our behalf and others. Get off the guilt and shame train about doing more and be brave enough to do less and rest in your identity in Christ and who HE says you are. Beloved, saved, redeemed, righteous, a child of the most High God. You are already approved of. Already loved. You don't have to earn this and you don't have to earn the approval of others. In fact it says in Galatians 1:10 "For am I now seeking the approval of man, or of God? Or am I trying to please man? If I were still trying to please man, I would not be a servant of Christ." Nothing can harm your marriage more then letting less important things take up time that could be spent together. It's there where the division happens. It happens slowly at first but before you know it there is a chasm between you and a lot of hobbies, activities and projects are what stand between you. Close the gap now and get back to the things that truly matter.

Father God, You are a God of order, not chaos. You are a God of peace not anxiety. In fact Your word says in 1 Peter 5:7 to cast our anxieties upon You because You care for us. It also says in Philippians 4:6 to be anxious for nothing. Will you show us where we need to cut things out that you aren't asking us to do and give us the courage to obey You quickly? Will You prioritize our time? Will You help us to be good stewards of the relationships You've entrusted to us, especially our marriage? We pray for our homes to be characterized by peace. We pray for You to be King over our homes and our hearts. We love You Lord and we praise You and thank You that You tell us Your burden is light and that You invite us to find rest in You. I pray that for each woman reading this right now. May she find rest in You Jesus, our Prince of Peace, in whose powerful name I ask these things, Amen.

WEEK 14
WHAT KIND OF CLOTHES SHOULD YOU WEAR FOR YOUR HUBBY?

I'm tricking you a bit with the title to entice you to read, but I think you'll find the clothes I'm talking about will be more meaningful than anything we will find in a store. I have been stuck in Colossians 3 for two weeks and the latest part I'm mulling over starts in verse 12 (NLT): "*Since God chose you to be the holy people he loves, you must clothe yourselves with…*"

-Tenderhearted mercy - Tenderhearted. It's easy to get hardened to our spouses when exhaustion takes over, apathy knocks at our door or over the years hurts get built up. Ezekiel 36:26 says, "And I will give you a new heart, and a new spirit I will put within you. And I will remove the heart of stone from your flesh and give you a heart of flesh." God can give you a new heart for your spouse. At ANY point! This should give us great hope for our marriages because none are hopeless with God with whom all things are possible (Matthew 19:26).

-Kindness- Kindness is a pre-requisite to a healthy marriage. My cousin went to a conference recently and one of the challenges was to be the best version of yourself at home. It's so easy to give our family our leftovers. But these are the most important relationships in our lives! These are the ones God entrusted to us to love and show His kindness and grace. In the days of showing our shiniest selves online, the challenge to be our best at home and consistently show kindness when the cameras are off is a timely one.

-Humility- It occurred to me yesterday that if every day we remembered the gospel, remembered what Christ really did for us, we would have no need to be "right" or make sure our way was *the* way. I woke up a couple mornings ago to Dom listening

to a sermon in the living room on Luke. The pastor was speaking about how Jesus was stripped with back, shoulders and buttocks exposed. Then He was beaten with a whip that literally ripped through his flesh. He was spat upon and mocked. I thought of His shame and His pain and how that was *my* beating He took. My only response was to kneel with tear-filled eyes and thank Him for paying for my sins with His very life. To thank Him for giving me an eternity with Him that I could never earn and for taking my guilt and my shame. It cost Him everything! If I could remember that every day, then I wouldn't be so high and mighty or entitled when it came to disagreements with Dominic (or anyone!). Instead, I would have a spirit of deep humility and gratitude and remember I am a sinner who was saved and shown infinite mercy, love and grace and it is my duty and obligation to extend that to everyone else, *especially* my one-flesh.

-Gentleness- Our words are powerful. We can hurt or help, build up or tear down. Treating others with gentleness in both word and deed is one of the most effective, loving things we can do. I also think it's one of the most Christ-like. He is the most powerful of all, yet Matthew 21:5 says, "See, your king comes to you, gentle and riding on a donkey." He is patient and gentle in His corrections, His teachings and His invitations. He has the power and authority to be as fierce as He wants, but so often He chooses gentleness with us and so should we with our spouse.

-Patience- Oh, how thankful I am that patience is a fruit of the Spirit and not something I can muster up in my own strength! The Lord has patience with us. He loves us with a never-ending, unfailing love and we would do our marriages a world of good to remember to be patient with our spouses by His power and trust that the Lord is working within them.

Aren't these just the most lovely garments imaginable to put on? Saks and Nieman Marcus can't even touch this! It doesn't end there though. Verse 13 says: *"Make allowance for each other's faults and forgive anyone who offends you. Remember the Lord forgave you."* Again, gospel. Let the gospel infiltrate every cell of your being. We can't possibly hold a grudge in light of the cross.

And last but not least, verses 14-15 say, "*Above all, clothe yourself with love, which binds us all together in perfect harmony. And let the peace that comes from Christ rule your hearts. For as members of one body you are called to live in peace. And always be thankful.*" Forgiveness. Love. Peace. Gratitude. The four pillars of a successful marriage. And love binds all of this together. It's the perfect, most important accessory and takes the outfit from mediocre to memorable. And we are called to live in peace as members of one body (the church), but as one-flesh even more! And there is always something we can be thankful for. Always. Having a hard time with this one? Start writing down the most basic things and watch how long that list becomes. Your salvation! Hot showers, food in your fridge, clean water, healthy kids, breath in your body, grass under your feet, your car that started this morning, the clothing you have for yourself and your family, the fact that you have more than one pair of shoes (or shoes at all!), access to medical help, friendships, family--you get the drift! Doesn't matter how big or small, write it down. See how differently you feel afterwards. Want to be an overachiever and put on your smarty pants with all these other clothes? Make a list of the things you are grateful for in your spouse.

The last part wasn't about clothing but it was too wonderful not to include. "*Let the message about Christ, in all its richness, fill your lives. Teach and counsel each other with all the wisdom He gives. Sing psalms and hymns and spiritual songs to God with thankful hearts and WHATEVER you do, do it as a representative of the Lord Jesus, giving thanks through Him to God the Father*" (Colossians 3:16-17 NLT [emphasis mine]). You are a representative of Christ in your marriage. One of our sweet praying wives told me this week that some of the things her husband had done were so hurtful, she was having a hard time getting past it. But the Lord keeps putting on her heart "love him." She was wrestling with this saying, "But Lord! He doesn't deserve it! He doesn't deserve my love! Look at how he is constantly hurting our marriage and breaking my heart!" Man, I think we have all felt that at some point! But the

Lord put on her heart that we do the same to Him. We turn to worthless idols instead of Him. We are unfaithful and break His heart yet He never stops loving us. We are to forgive because we are forgiven. We are to love because He loves us. We are to be His representatives because we died with Him and it is no longer we who live, but Christ who lives in us (Galatians 2:20).

Now let me end with this warning. If you try and put on these clothes by yourself every morning, you're going to end up looking like my two-year-old. He either has just a shirt on and no pants, my husband's shoes (and nothing else), or is just plain naked all the time #truestory. Just like this toddler, we don't have what it takes to consistently dress appropriately. Left to our own devices, we put on selfish sweaters and judgmental jeggings. Or we walk around stark naked! We NEED our Heavenly Father to lovingly dress us as a parent dresses a helpless child. It's only by His power and grace that we can be clothed in a way that will bless others. So! Tomorrow morning when you wake up, ask Him to dress you! And watch your marriage change before your eyes as He works out these characteristics in your life.

Be blessed, Warrior Wives. Be strengthened by Him. Love with His love. Forgive with His grace. You are loved. Fiercely. He was slapped, spit upon, beaten and murdered so that we could be with Him forever. One of my favorite songs says, "He didn't want heaven without us." Makes me cry like a freakin baby every time. We have an eternity of bliss to look forward to and in the meantime, He will give us His Holy Spirit to empower us to put on each of these "pieces of clothing" so that we will be women of true beauty for our husbands in our marriages. These clothes will always be in style and will fit no matter what kind of dessert we had last night.

Lord Jesus, thank You for taking our beating. Thank You for taking our guilt and shame and paying for our sin so we can have an eternity with You. If that weren't enough, You offer Yourself to us daily so we don't have to go it alone. You also offer us these beautiful "garments" that help us be more like You. Father, as Your little girls we come to You and ask our Heavenly Daddy to clothe us. May we walk around with tenderhearted mercy, kindness, humility, gentleness, patience, love and peace so that those around us will truly experience Your likeness because YOU are all of these beautiful things. May our spouses see You in us and may our inward beauty shine the most to them as a result of what You do in our hearts. They are Yours. We love You so much. In Jesus' name, Amen.

WEEK 15
MISMATCHED SEX DRIVES

Dominic and I were watching a sermon series on Song of Solomon that has been like attending marriage counseling (this is the link to the video and audio: http://marshill.se/marshill/media/the-peasant-princess). First, if you ever get a chance to watch a sermon with your hubby at home, not just at church, it is life changing. I can't encourage it enough. Find a biblically sound pastor you both enjoy and watch together while playing a game or instead of a movie!

Something I liked about this series is that he gives questions for you and your spouse to ask each other after the sermon. This has prompted many conversations for us that I think we could have avoided for a lifetime. One such question was, "How often should you make love with your spouse?" There are different answers for everyone but the overall idea is to figure out what you are both comfortable with and to not deprive one another. Paul writes in 1 Corinthians 5:7, "Do not deprive one another, except perhaps by agreement for a limited time, that you may devote yourselves to prayer; but then come together again, so that Satan may not tempt you because of your lack of self-control."

There are many factors that play a part in desire that are different for every one including: stress, sickness, new babies, issues in the marriage, history of abuse, different sex drives, etc.
The different sex drives was interesting because as women, we tend to desire sex less (although that's not always the case!). I stumbled on a great article about this exact issue that I encourage you to check out: http://www.imom.com/mismatched-sex-drives-and-what-you-can-do-about-it/#.V8SH08T3anM

Another great reference for a possible lack of desire is a book called *Lucy Libido Says.....There's an Oil for THAT: A Girlfriend's Guide to Using Essential Oils Between the Sheets*. It is both hilarious and extremely informative and addresses our lack of desire (or his!)

from several different points (including hormone imbalances) with some real application tips to improve the quality of your sex life.

Different sex drives can be a huge conflict in our marriages, to the point that it can lead to infidelity and divorce. Sex is an important part of your marriage and God created us to have physical needs that are to be beautifully met by only our spouses. 1 Corinthians 7:4 says, "For the wife does not have authority over her own body, but the husband does. Likewise the husband does not have authority over his own body, but the wife does." Now this is not a verse to be used for abuse! I know that can happen and it breaks my heart that men would compromise their wives based on desire. But it also breaks my heart that women would withhold sex from their husband as a means of control or to use every excuse in the book to avoid it just because they don't feel like it. We need to be sensitive to one another in this area because guess what: only you can meet this need for your spouse. No one else! It's important for spouses to love each other in a physical way and to decide upon together what you both feel comfortable with in terms of how often. We avoid these conversations but they can be so healing. A healthy sex life will do absolute wonders for your marriage. Working together to figure out how to properly balance your sex drive with your spouse might be one of the most important things you ever do as a couple.

And while we're on the topic, when was the last time you initiated making love to your spouse? As I mentioned earlier, often (although not always), men tend to have a higher sex drive and initiate way more then women. But as a man, can you imagine how good it would feel if their wife showed desire first? It would be a huge confidence booster to him to know you wanted him in that way and a huge bonding experience in reminding each other how important that connection is not only physically but mentally and spiritually as well.

One of the wives a couple meetings back said she'd been struggling in the area of "wanting to." I think we've all been there! We are tired and often the last thing we feel like at the end of the day is to exert more energy or be touched. But! Her solution was so awesome I had to share it. She said she knew it was becoming a difficult area in their marriage so she started praying during the day for the Lord to increase her desire and bless their time together that night. I thought this was brilliant first of all because we often forget to invite the Lord into this beautiful thing He created. Anything He is a part of will automatically be better! Second, women usually take a lot longer to become aroused then men. I heard this hilarious analogy that men are like a light switch and women are like all the complicated electrical work behind it. To start thinking of this early on with a sensual text or just mentally preparing can do wonders in this department.

I know this isn't always easy! In total transparency, sometimes I get shy! I imagine I will be all confident and sexy and put on lingerie or have music playing and candles burning but then I'll chicken out because I feel vulnerable putting myself out there. Or I'll put on that negligee and "think where did that patch of cellulite come from? Nursing that third child did nothing for your perkiness girlfriend!" I even threw my back out once trying to arch in a sexy way on the couch and ended up crawling away in pain saying "don't look at me! Don't look at me!" Boy was that an awkward visit to the chiropractor.

But hear me on this: they DO NOT CARE. They will be thrilled they don't have to ask and even more thrilled you are changing things up a bit and showing them they are wanted and desired. Who doesn't want to feel like that?

On the other end if you have the higher sex drive, you may have painfully experienced rejection. I don't want to be insensitive to that! Regardless of how he responds, I think it means something that we show them we are interested and want to prioritize making love. And adding prayer to that mix can only help things because prayer helps everything. On that note, I also want to caution you if you are the one doing the rejecting. That can hurt a man really deeply and cause wounds over time. I know sometimes you might not be feeling well but some of the healthiest marriages I know do not make a regular habit of denying one another.

Anyway, hoping to challenge you this week to have a conversation about this and maybe even to plan a sensual night! It can be as simple as walking out of the bathroom naked (be careful of sexy arching) or as complicated as planning a night away for just the two of you. Just do your part to make it a priority and something you both can talk about. I'm always shocked by how much closer I feel to Dom afterwards and how much more connected we are. It literally reminds us we are one and that we are a team.

Father God, thank You for the gift of sex. Thank you that it literally represents the one-flesh design You desire for us and helps us feel closer to our husbands not only physically but mentally and spiritually as well. We pray You would facilitate some healthy conversations with our husbands and that You would help us come to a place where we both feel satisfied in this area. We pray that You would help us come to You with this issue more, and that we would recognize that You can do a mighty work in this important part of our marriage if put in Your hands. We ask Your forgiveness for the times we have withheld intimacy from our spouse in any way due to our own selfishness or control. We want to glorify You in this area of our lives and need Your help to do just that. In Jesus' name we pray, Amen.

WEEK 16
COUPLES WHO PRAY
TOGETHER STAY TOGETHER

Our dear friends, the Birches, said the best marriage advice they ever got was that couples who pray together, stay together. Without fail, this couple starts each morning in Bible study and prayer together ("Listen to my voice in the morning, Lord. Each morning I bring my requests to you and wait expectantly." Psalm 5:3 NLT). They've been married for decades, run a business together, are rock solid and give the Lord all the credit!

Here is another challenge: let's commit to pray with our spouse at least once this week. It sounds simple and for some of you it might be something you already do every day. If this isn't the case, don't feel badly about it! This can be awkward at first. In fact, one of my favorite pastors talked about this in a sermon a while back. He said as a man he didn't want to sound dumb in front of his wife or even be super vulnerable, but as they continued praying together, over time it became one of the most intimate acts of their marriage.

I was reminded of this one day when I felt an overwhelming need to pray with Dom. He came home from work and looked exhausted. I had a cold and wasn't feeling too well myself so I hesitated to bring it up because it would have just been easier to pick out a movie and not talk. However, the Holy Spirit convicted me and Dominic said, "You know, it's been little while since we've prayed together and I've been feeling that way too."

By the end of us taking turns praying, I genuinely felt so much closer to him and so much peace over all the things that were troubling me beforehand once we purposefully came together to focus on Christ. It put all of our issues in perspective and reminded me of the verse in Isaiah 26:3 that says "You keep him in perfect peace whose mind is stayed on you, because he trusts in you."

It's a small act with huge consequences not only in your lives, but the heavenlies. I'm fully aware that this might be new for you or him or both, so maybe you could ask and if he seems uncomfortable, you could just offer to pray for him? Sometimes it's difficult for people to pray out loud. I know that took getting used to for Dominic because he said he was used to just talking to God on his own, not in front of someone else. However, over the years, this has become not only comfortable but a common part of our daily lives and is now some of our most treasured times together.

Pray for the courage and time to ask him and don't have too many expectations if this is new. Starting something is always hard at first but this is something that you will be glad you did!

We thank You, Jesus Christ, for tearing the veil that day You sacrificed Your life for us on the cross. As a result we can now boldly come before the throne and pray with Your righteousness covering us head to toe. We pray that You would increase our desire to pray and that You would help us learn how to pray with our husbands. As we seek to draw closer to You and closer to each other, we know that's a prayer You will answer. Please give us the courage and opportunity this week to bow before You, our King, as one-flesh. We praise You for the privilege of prayer and the privilege of marriage. In Your powerful name, Amen.

WEEK 17
MARRIAGE MASTERS VS. DISASTERS

I stumbled on an article over the weekend and had to share its findings. John Gottman is a psychologist who has devoted most of his life to studying relationships and whether or not they will stay together. According to him, he can predict with 94 percent certainty whether couples—straight or gay, rich or poor, childless or not—will be broken up, together and unhappy, or together and happy several years later. There are masters and disasters and much of it comes down to the spirit couples bring to the relationship. Do they bring kindness and generosity; or contempt, criticism, and hostility? (see more here: https://www.theatlantic.com/health/archive/2014/06/happily-ever-after/372573/)[1]

I love how often a "discovery" in science only proves biblical principles. If we showed the kindness and generosity towards our spouse that Christ shows to us, our marriages would not only survive but most likely flourish. As I type this, several faces popped in my mind that are truly struggling right now and the thought probably crossed your mind, "Well he isn't kind or generous to me, so why should I be to him? He makes it so hard to be kind!" Even if our spouse isn't doing the same, Romans 2:4 says, "Or do you presume on the riches of his kindness and forbearance and patience, not knowing that God's kindness is meant to lead you to repentance?" Our kindness (which does not and should not depend on theirs) can actually lead to repentance. Another verse that comes to mind is 1 Peter 3:1, "Likewise, wives, be subject to your own husbands, so that even if some do not obey the word, they may be won without a word by the conduct of their wives." Our behavior can influence them infinitely more than our nagging or defeating words.

Are we being generous and kind? Or are we eye-rolling, speaking with condescension dripping from our tongues or pointing out all they are doing wrong instead of all they are doing right?

This is a silly example, but this morning I found some batteries in the laundry room. I needed some for Boaz' favorite toy so Dom told me he would get some. This is not a criticism but full disclosure, he often forgets little things like this. Owning a business requires a lot of brain power and attention to a lot of details so I get that (most of the time! Ha!). But a couple weeks ago, I had asked him to bring home a certain tool I needed and he kept forgetting. I took it as a personal offense and thought to myself he must think me unimportant and never listens. Discovering those unexpected batteries today revealed the lies from Satan I was believing. He jumps in there so fast to turn us against our spouses. Think about it. When our relationships with our husbands suffer, everything else does too. Our health (mental, physical and spiritual), our children's sense of well-being and security, our jobs, ministries, other relationships...if he can attack our one-flesh relationship, he inadvertently attacks lots of other areas with one swoop.

Shut those lies DOWN! Pray often for Jesus to expose any lies you are believing and replace them with truth. Look for a reminder today of the good in your husband. You married him for a reason. If you're having a hard time, pray for the Lord to show you some "batteries" or bring to mind something you love and respect about him. And then tell him! Text, email, call, or wait till tonight when you see him face to face, but tell him. Unfortunately in marriage we forget to encourage each other. We forget to show kindness and generosity. The amazing thing about kindness is that it's a fruit of the Spirit which means it comes from Him. His Spirit. You don't have to muster this up on your own.

Lord, will You fill us with Your kindness and generosity so we can overflow this onto our husbands? We didn't deserve Your love when You showed it to us while we were still sinners and You died for us (Romans 5:8), so we pray that even when they don't "deserve" it, we can still love them because of the example You gave for us. May we die to ourselves so You can live through us. May we be filled with Your strength and conviction to tell them when they love us well or help us.

May we be changed so our marriages can be changed by Your love and grace. In Jesus' name, Amen.

EMAIL 18
WOULD YOU WANT TO BE
MARRIED TO YOU?

One of our teaching pastors at church posed an interesting question on Sunday: Would you want to be married to you?

It was convicting. In my own life I thought sometimes yes and sometimes no. I often let exhaustion or hormones or just plain sin get the better of me and poor Dom doesn't know if he's coming home to a clean, welcoming home with dinner on the table, worship music playing, and essential oils diffusing or a frazzled wife with cold leftovers and an apocalyptic living room. He's always so consistently pleasant with me it makes me want to be that way towards him more.

I think often we show our friends more love and grace than our own husbands. What if we treated them more like best friends? Technically they should be our best friend anyway, and although we might claim that verbally, our actions speak otherwise. If I treated him as kindly as I did my bestie, I would indeed want to be married to me. Below is an excerpt from Michael Hyatt's blog for three practical steps on how to be your spouse's best friend (side note: he's a great resource for business, productivity, writing, etc.! Can't recommend him enough!):

"Step 1. Make a List of What You Would Want in a Best Friend
If you were going to advertise on Craigslist for a best friend, what would the ad look like? Perhaps it might look like this:

Wanted: Best Friend
Prospective candidates will:

Make me feel good about being me.

Affirm my best qualities (especially when I am feeling insecure).

Call out the best in me, and hold me accountable to the best version of myself.

Listen without judging or trying to fix me.

Give me the benefit of the doubt.

Extend grace to me when I am grumpy or having a bad day.

Remember my birthday, favorite foods, music, and art.

Know my story and love me regardless.

Spend time with me, just because they enjoy my company.

Speak well of me when I am not present.

Serve me with a joyful spirit and without complaining.

Speak the truth to me when no one else will.

Never shame me, diminish me, or make me feel small.

Become excited about what I am excited about.

Celebrate my wins!

Step 2. Now Become That Person for Your Spouse
That's right. Turn the table. Make this a list of the kind of friend you will become. I can promise you this: anyone who does half of these kinds of things will have more friends than he or she knows what to do with. But what if you focused this effort on your spouse? Think of the possibilities. Psychologist John Gottman has spent years researching what makes some marriages flourish and others fall apart. He found lasting relationships comes down to friendship. Couples who stay married make an intentional effort to connect, share interests, and meet their spouse's emotional needs.

Step 3. Keep Sowing the Seeds Until the Relationship Blossoms
How long will it take to create this kind of relationship? It all depends on where you are starting. For some, it might be several months. For others, it might take years. Friendships are like gardens; they must be cultivated. The key is to be consistent and persistent—without expectations. There's usually reason to hope in almost any circumstance. "[T]here's a great deal of evidence showing the more someone receives or witnesses kindness, the

more they will be kind themselves, which leads to upward spirals of love and generosity in a relationship," says Emily Esfhani Smith. It's amazing what can happen when we assume the best and stay meaningfully engaged with our spouses. This is really nothing more than the application of the Golden Rule to marriage: "'Do to others what you would want them to do to you' (Luke 6:31). If couples would invest in one another like I am suggesting, the divorce rate would plummet. Romance is important. Sex is too. But a solid friendship is the foundation of everything else."
-Michael Hyatt [1]

I read this out loud to Dominic when he got home and asked him afterwards how I could be a better friend to him. It was a cool discussion and I thought it would be a great question for you to ask your hubbies this week and also a great prayer for them. They might not share anything specifically but God will give us insight into how to do this if we ask Him.

Lord, thank You for marriage. It is beautiful and mysterious and an adventure when put safely in the palms of Your hands. Since You are the Creator of marriage, there is no other place we should put it. We thank You for the gift of friendship and that marriage can actually be the ultimate friendship. We pray You would cultivate that in our marriages by Your grace. By Your strength, would You help us be the ones to start giving more generously and serving more sacrificially? We love You and thank You and ask this in the powerful name of Jesus Christ. Amen.

EMAIL 19
COMING INTO AGREEMENT

We were in Minnesota on vacation visiting Spencer's parents. It's never lost on me what a special bond we have; that the parents of my first husband who passed away suddenly have remained a constant, steady force in our lives. They not only prayed for me to remarry but when I met Dominic, they said they weren't losing a daughter but gaining a son and immediately flew us all up to meet him. Dominic fell in love with them and the close bond we already enjoyed only got stronger. We continue to fly up every year and our blended, beautiful family prays together and laughs together and I leave in tears every time because I know how much I'll miss them. I've mentioned them many times in this group because as you can see, they are very special people. They have been married over 40 years and are marriage coaches in a ministry called "Married for Life" (This ministry offers online courses and interactive courses with coaching for any stage of your marriage and can be accessed at this website https://www.2equal1.com/courses/courses/married-for-life/).

One of the things my "mother-in-love" Pam mentioned a few times while we were there was the term "coming into agreement." I asked her to elaborate on what she meant by that and couldn't wait to share what she said.

When faced with a decision, it's imperative to come into agreement with your spouse before going forward. God isn't a God of confusion and will guide you when you ask Him. Coming into agreement starts by praying and seeking the Lord together and then checking in with each other asking "what did God tell you?"

This is important because you can't blame each other if you've come to a decision together. If you both have differing opinions about something, you need to seek the Lord together so He can put you on the same page, HIS page. This helps you stay in His will and protects you from resentment and anger. It can prevent bad decisions about your finances, job, your children, etc. You are one flesh and want to be on the same page because in marriage you are a team, an "us." A "we." In the Bible there are multiple verses on the topic of unity (ex: "I appeal to you, brothers, by the name of our Lord Jesus Christ, that all of you agree, and that there be no divisions among you, but that you be united in the same mind and the same judgment." 1 Corinthians 1:10) It makes all the more sense that if you are one -flesh He would want you to be united and on the same page, but isn't it merciful and sweet of Him to do that for us when we can't? And to do it in a way that as unique individuals we will hear from Him?

Something I noticed the Greenlees did every morning over coffee and breakfast was to get in the word together (even if it was just a couple of verses) and they always prayed over their day and asked God what He wanted them to do. They said when they take care of God's business, He takes care of their business. Sometimes they will go into a day thinking they will do this or that but the Lord will put on their hearts something completely different. Many times in retrospect, they will see how important and timely the thing He put on their heart was to do. Since He is the Creator of the universe and is sovereign, He knows what is coming and can equip us and prepare us for not just the big decisions, but our day to day agendas. Hebrews 13:21 (NLT) says, "May he equip you with all you need for doing his will. May he produce in you, through the power of Jesus Christ, every good thing that is pleasing to him. All glory to him forever and ever! Amen."

An example of this is my brother in law, Kevin. He was the head of a catering company and was doing well but when he and his wife Holly went away for a weekend with several of their friends to a bed and breakfast, Kevin felt this overwhelming desire to open a B&B of his own. Now Holly is extremely practical. She has worked for the same company for 25 years and is excellent with money. For them to take on such an endeavor it was critical for them to come into agreement. After much prayer together, they believed they should move forward. It wasn't an easy process! They had to sell their home, find a location for the B&B, pass zoning laws, get permits, remodel, advertise, invest money, etc. But because they were in agreement, they were able to go forward with confidence and because Holly is a part of this, they are in it together. Kevin isn't going to resent Holly for not getting to realize this dream and Holly isn't going to resent Kevin if it doesn't work out because they assessed the risks together and agreed to move forward in the direction God was guiding them. Looking back on his life, it was as if the Lord had prepared Kevin for this very thing. Even jobs that didn't make sense at the time suddenly did. I honestly have never seen them happier.

When seeking the Lord together, remember that one of the primary ways He speaks to us is in His word. Nothing the Lord guides us to do will ever contradict scripture but only confirm it. If seeking counsel together, remember to go to someone who is biblically sound and trusted. When you both want to do the Lord's will, He will always meet you there because He wants you in His will even more then you do!

Father in Heaven, Your word says if we delight ourselves in You, that You will give us the desires of our hearts (Psalm 37:4). We pray that as a married couple we would delight ourselves in You. We pray we would remember You are sovereign and that You know what is coming and what is best for us. We pray we would lay down our pride and focus on You so our hearts and minds are ripe and open to hear from You. Please keep us on the same page with each other and with You. We ask this boldly in the name of Christ whose righteousness covers us, Amen.

EMAIL 20
WEATHERING THE STORM:
STRESS AND YOUR MARRIAGE

My topic this week is: How do we deal with *outside* stressors so that they don't become stressors *inside* our marriage? No seriously. I'm asking you. Write to me right now if you have a solution.

I'm kidding. Sort of. I do have some tips but this is coming from someone who has had to apply these tips like crazy this past year and if I'm totally being honest, I've been needing to apply them a bit this morning too. With the direct hit of category 4 Hurricane Irma all the while being 40 weeks pregnant, things have been tense!

Stress is no joke. There are many studies that suggest it's a leading cause of disease and when we are under it, it can definitely affect us not only physically, but relationally. Our irritability tends to increase, our tones become less kind, out of fear or worry we can lash out on the people we love, and it can inhibit intimacy--just to name a few things.

With a baby who is overdue, moving three times in the past week due to the hurricane, the emotional roller coaster of figuring out what was important enough to pack and what wasn't with a possible flood surge, wondering if we should evacuate or stay put, choosing to ride out the storm so we wouldn't risk giving birth on the side of the highway, dealing with no electricity and water issues, watching the devastation of your town--and throw on some huge financial stress due to lack of work for the indefinite future--well, it's been stressful.

And you don't need a hurricane for that! So many of the women I know have faced some incredibly difficult things this year ranging from losing jobs, moving homes, deaths in the family, financial strain, new additions to the family (which are wonderful but also stressful!), damage to homes, sickness, in-law issues, etc. None of these are technically marital stressors but they can cause stress to your marriage because these things drain you emotionally and physically. And at the end of the day we are human! As much as we know these things aren't our spouses' fault, because they are the closest person to us, they tend to receive the brunt of our frustration and anxiety and we tend to receive theirs.

SO! How do we deal with this? How do we stay Christ-like to our husbands (and others!) when everything in our flesh wants to react?

Here are ten tips:

1. Take time to be with God! I know this is hard when you have no alone time and if you're in stifling heat right now because you're still out of electricity it's even harder! But even if it's a trip to the bathroom with a closed door and a prayer or a hymn of praise while washing dishes, just take a minute to be quiet before Him, ask Him to fill you with His strength and peace and love to the point that it overflows.

2. Take a deep breath (or 10) before you say something you might regret. It's not sinful to be angry, but it's how we react to that anger that becomes sin. You can't take back words and they can hurt worse than anything else.

3. Remember you're on the same team. It might not feel like it sometimes with differing opinions and ways of doing things, but you made a covenant with him before God which automatically makes you one. There is no him. There is no you. There is only a "we" so remind yourself of that as often as you need to (and remind him of that too! Sometimes it makes all the difference in the world to tell him, "Hey! I'm on your side! No matter what!").

4. Pray together. It will put you on the same page and give you perspective in a stressful situation.

5. Take care of yourselves. As much as you can, get the sleep, exercise and nutrition you need to be able to function well. Not eating, exercising, or sleeping well only compounds the stress you are already dealing with.

6. Figure out a way to laugh together! Crack a joke, make light of a situation, make a funny face and catch him off guard... laughter immediately reduces stress in your body and is very bonding!

7. Don't neglect intimacy if you can help it. It's important to come together in times of stress and hardship even when sometimes it's the last thing you feel like doing. It connects you in a way very little else can and again, reminds you in a tangible way that you are one.

8. Give each other grace and be quick to forgive. People don't act like themselves under severe stress. If he is quieter than normal, angrier than normal, more distant, etc. remember this is not his norm! Or yours! I've had to apologize many a time this past week for being so quick to snap or cry out of frustration or fear and he has been very quick to forgive and show me grace (and vice versa although he has had way less breakdowns than me! #pregnancyhormones).

9. Be honest about what you're struggling with and ask him what he's struggling with. Usually men and women have very different concerns and priorities and they are ALL important. This week Dom was worried about plywood and flashlights and I was more worried about giving birth in a storm and having enough food for the boys. You should have more conversations than normal when under stress although the temptation is to have less. Try to over-communicate if necessary so you can learn to focus on these things together instead of separately.

10. Remember this too shall pass. Focus on getting through this hour, this day, with the strength of the Lord and that all

things are possible with Him (Matthew 19:26). Sometimes it feels like our worlds are crashing around us, but we won't always be in this place. Focusing too far in the future about what may or may not happen only adds to our stress level and the Lord wants us to focus on Him and the things above (Colossians 3:2). Make His business your business and He will make your business His business. He is not asking you to go through this alone but to take each step while holding His hand and receiving His love and strength.

Lord, thank You that even under stress your grace is sufficient for us. Thank You that You will ALWAYS help us and supply us with the peace that surpasses understanding no matter what our circumstances are. Give us Your perspective, Lord. Help us supernaturally understand that our husbands might be dealing with things we don't understand and give us grace to the point that we can overflow it onto them. We ask that in these stressful situations we would actually grow closer to you and closer to one another instead of apart. We praise You and thank You that all things are possible with You. It's in Jesus' powerful name we pray. Amen.

EMAIL 21
ACCOUNTABILITY

Does your man have accountability to anyone? Do you?

Not just a group of friends that will tell you what you want to hear but someone who will speak truth to you, even if it's going to hurt. I can think of at least three marriages off the top of my head that had they had someone in their lives whom they were being honest with, and who was being honest with them back, could have been warned that the path they were headed down was dangerous.

This is not a real example so don't try and imagine who I'm talking about but let's just say "Alex" started carpooling with a coworker named "Sheila" to save gas. Seemed innocent but over time, an inappropriate relationship was formed. Both were committed in their marriages but the excess time together allowed for a sharing of emotions and feelings that led to an affair.

Had Alex talked about the situation with a godly man, or Sheila with a godly woman, more than likely that person would have said, "Hey, this isn't a good idea. You're playing with fire here. Find another way to work."

The reason we need accountability is that we are lied to from the moment we wake up to the moment we go to bed: by Satan, our own thoughts, by TV, the radio, and the people around us. We need to constantly be exposed to truth in order to recognize those lies. The primary accountability in our lives should be scripture: "For the word of God is living and active, sharper than any two-edged sword, piercing to the division of soul and of spirit, of joints and of marrow, and discerning the thoughts and intentions of the heart." (Hebrews 4:12).

But we also need a community of believers and someone who is strong in the Word of God that we can be truly transparent with.

Now don't go freaking out if you don't have this or your husband doesn't have this. Start praying for it! First of all, this group is hopefully a safe place for you to seek counsel and prayer. But pray for an older woman in your life that will speak the truth of God's word to you regularly and who will lovingly point out things that don't edify your life or a lie that needs to be replaced with truth. And if your husband doesn't have this, start praying for that too, for a godly man he can respect and be honest with. "Iron sharpens iron, and one man sharpens another." (Proverbs 27:17).

I'm not saying they have to meet every week but pray that the person God brings along for yourself or your spouse or both would have the desire and discipline to seek you out and give you regular time to listen, counsel, and pray with and for you. And also, give back. You might be that person for someone else too! The best thing you can do right now is to stay strong in your study of God. Read His word, listen to His word, listen to sermons from pastors who are sound in their biblical theology during the week, read books from authors who are biblically focused, get involved in a church and especially get involved in a Bible study or small group. Hebrews 10:25 says, "And let us consider how to stir up one another to love and good works, not neglecting to meet together, as is the habit of some, but encouraging one another, and all the more as you see the Day drawing near."

Fill your mind with truth! Be around others who will fill your mind with truth! And speak truth lovingly but boldly to others!

Lord Jesus, thank You that You ARE TRUTH. And that You set us free. And that You are more powerful than the one who lies to us and accuses us. Lord, please give us and our husbands people that we can be accountable to. People that will lovingly speak truth to us and warn us about going down a path that would lead us towards danger. Please bring people into our lives who will pray for us and counsel us and, Lord, help us be that for others. We love you and trust You, Jesus. Give us a hunger for Your word like never before. Please protect and bless our marriages in the way only You can. We trust ourselves and our husbands into Your care. In Your powerful name, Jesus, we pray.

EMAIL 22
THE TRUTH ABOUT DIVORCE

On the way home one night, I turned on the radio and there was a woman speaking about the pain of her divorce. She sounded exactly like Miss Clara from the movie "War Room" (side note, if you haven't seen that, put that at the TOP of your to-do list. It is life-changing, marriage-altering, amazing). Her actual name was Patricia Ashley and she said the most intriguing thing: "Why doesn't anyone talk about how truly painful divorce is? I mean, if you're divorced, that should be our full-time job. Going around to other troubled marriages and telling them that divorce will rip your heart in two and hurt everyone around you and that it's not worth it and do whatever it takes to work it out. I mean, someone should warn them! No one could have prepared me for the pain that my divorce would cause."[1] Her message was an incredible one. She got remarried and the same problems that she had in her first marriage were there again in her second marriage and she felt like that one was going to die too. I put the podcast below because it talked about how God brought her marriage back to life when she had no hope. You can find it here:

http://www.focusonthefamily.com/media/daily-broadcast/experiencing-a-fulfilled-marriage-pt1

It got me thinking about all the lies we hear about divorce. "We will be better off." "It will be better for the kids to have two parents that aren't fighting even if that means not being married anymore." "We just grew apart. We don't love each other anymore." Etc, etc. The lies are only exacerbated in the media with movies and TV glorifying divorce and making it seem as though it were no bigger a deal than changing sofas. But they ARE lies because it is the ripping of two souls a part. As a child of divorce, I never wanted to get married for fear of the intense pain that I knew would be the result if there was a divorce. My mom and dad are incredible parents and grandparents and I would never presume to understand or judge what happened in their marriage. But the divorce definitely affected my siblings and I in different ways and it is still difficult years later with grandchildren and holidays that must be split up.

Bottom line, I just couldn't help but think Patricia was right. Why don't we talk about how bad it is? Do you know anyone who is divorced? Are they happy? Honestly? Did their divorce really help their children for the better? I'm sure there are some rare exceptions but for the most part, I think the vast majority would answer "no." I'm not coming from a place of judgment or feeling like I know best, but the Bible is really onto something (no kidding!). We are to love our spouses with *agape* (unconditional love) and offer the same forgiveness that Christ extends to us. There is no greater way to live out the gospel than within our own marriages. There is no greater example of the gospel then to forgive our spouses and stay married because that in and of itself is a tangible example of the covenant He made with us. We are His no matter what. He forgives us and loves us no matter what. And there is such comfort in knowing He isn't going anywhere. He wants us to offer that same grace to our spouse because it's in that promise where someone can really feel safe. Now I know we aren't married to Jesus. We are married to imperfect people who hurt us (and we hurt them!), but that is where we really get to apply this. We get to ask for God's strength to forgive and to love. And we get to let Him be our defender against the hurts that are caused. He WILL help you. Wherever and whatever state your marriage is in, He can breathe life back into it.

I wrestled with whether to write this or not because it's such a sensitive subject and few people have *not* been affected by divorce. But I always pray God would give me wisdom and content for each email and I really feel as though He led me to do this. We have to do everything we can to avoid divorce. Imagine being in a room with no doors. That is your marriage. You are in it! Spencer and I joked that everyone should be forced to live in a 32-foot Airstream their first year of marriage like we were. If you fight, you have nowhere to go so you have to work it out!

Romans 15:13 (NLT) says "I pray that God, the source of hope, will fill you completely with joy and peace because you trust in him. Then you will overflow with confident hope through the power of the Holy Spirit." Let hope prevail! When trouble and pain press in on every side, many couples become depressed and deceived by the feeling that there is no hope but that's because they aren't looking to the only source of hope: God! They are tricked by the frequently quoted (but incorrect!)[2] idea that half of all marriages end in divorce. They worry, "If half of all the other marriages can't make it, what makes us so special?" and they give up as their courage slips away due to a lie that is tailor-made to steal our hope.

Don't let it. This miraculous institution that God has created to mirror the relationship between us and Jesus still works. He is still working. You can trust in Him, even when you cannot trust yourself or your spouse. But you must live in that hope! Even if you are the only one clinging to that hope – CLING. You must walk in the faith of things not yet seen, doing what you are called to do, as if the answer is guaranteed. The power of our hope in Him is so transformative, so life-giving that if even one partner is fighting for the marriage, if even one person won't give up, if even one person does what they can do regardless of whether their spouse does the same... it is absolutely possible for that marriage to survive and most likely thrive.

If you need help with your marriage, get in the word first and foremost and pray to "God , the source of hope." Find a biblical counselor to help you or look into getting a coach through the Married for Life Ministry[3]. They also have classes called "Married for Life" that you can take from the privacy of your own home via computer. These are incredible and have helped so many other couples. They can be found here: https://www.2equal1.com

Dear Lord, give me the courage and hope I need for the rich and beautiful marriage you want for me. Please protect us from divorce. Show me where I have been believing the lies of discouragement, and open my eyes to the truth. In the weeks to come, help me to see exactly

how to apply these biblical principles to my own marriage and do what I can do-- and to watch as You do the great things that only You can do. Amen

EMAIL 23
LESS OF YOU

My friend Kim Shepson created a Bible study on the book of John that I've been working through. Today's lesson was out of John 3:28-30 when John the Baptist said, "You yourselves bear me witness, that I said, 'I am not the Christ, but I have been sent before him.' The one who has the bride is the bridegroom. The friend of the bridegroom, who stands and hears him, rejoices greatly at the bridegroom's voice. Therefore this joy of mine is now complete. He must increase, but I must decrease." Her question was, "How would your relationships change if they were governed by the growing desire that 'Jesus must increase, I must decrease?'"

I thought about this question just in general and how freeing it would be if this were my constant mindset, to be less self-focused and more others-focused. Then I thought about it in regards to specific relationships and of course the ones on the front of my mind were my marriage and my kids. Her next question really convicted me regarding these: "In our relationships, do people see more of us or more of God? What do they think about when they walk away?"

It's easier for me to be Christ-like to people I don't see very often. It doesn't require as much energy to do it for a short period or to put your "best face forward" so to speak. But in marriage, your spouse sees all your faces! I thought about when my husband leaves in the morning and "walks away" like the question stated. Did my actions that morning show him the love of Jesus? Did my words the night before encourage and edify him or were they grumbles, complaints or discouraging remarks?

In marriage, we often give our spouse the worst version of ourselves and end up giving everyone else the best version because we don't see the other people so much. In order to give our spouses the best version, we need to be intentional about it, otherwise they get the exhausted left-overs. I think this requires more than just intentionality, however. It requires prayer and the strength of Jesus in us because, let's be honest, the ins and outs of our daily life take a lot out of us! I often feel like I'm running on fumes by the time he gets home and even if I'm intending to be the "best wife in the world" when he crosses that threshold, all my good intentions can just go down the drain without the strength and love of Christ filling me up to overflow onto him.

Lord, less of us, more of You. That's our heart's cry. We want the most important earthly relationship we have, which is with our spouse, to be one where You shine through us to them. When I think of who You are, You are humble, a servant, a warrior, One who sacrifices Yourself out of love for others. May we, by the power of Your Spirit, emulate You to our husbands. We lift them up to you, Lord. We pray Your blessing and protection over them and over our marriages. We pray for Your strength in our weakness. You are our hope, Lord, and it's in You we trust. We commit these things to You in the powerful name of Jesus Christ. Amen.

EMAIL 24
HOW YOU WERE RAISED

How was your husband raised? How were you? Did your parents have a good marriage? Did they model what being a good husband/ wife or father/mother was?

I had this epiphany listening to someone's marriage struggles the other day. As she was talking, I was suddenly reminded of what her husband's dad was like. Who is a total jerk by the way. Sorry. I shouldn't say that but dude... He's mean, derogatory, judgmental, on his third or fourth marriage and has greatly hurt his son over the years with how he talks to him because honestly it's the closest thing to verbal abuse that I can imagine. Now the son he raised is married. He and his wife are having problems. Well, duh! Not that we have to repeat the cycle but if the son never learned how to do this, never saw what a good husband or dad looked like and since then hasn't gone out of his way to learn (or unlearn) what he saw, the cycle often *is* repeated because we haven't replaced those bad habits with good. We haven't replaced the lies with truth.

Right before I met Spencer, The Lord in His grace put a lot of people who had healthy marriages in my life. I became curious and #readallthemarriagebooks because I knew if I was going to do this marriage thing, I would never be able to handle the heartbreak of divorce. Dominic had a similar experience. Although he wanted to get married, he was also a child of divorce so he watched #allthemarriagesermons and found some people who had healthy marriages and spent time with them, asking the husbands what it took to be married happily and how to be a good husband and dad.

Here's the thing. He may need help! *You* may need help! We aren't born hardwired knowing how to be good spouses. A lot of the problems you might be experiencing aren't either one of you intentionally hurting each other but might be the repeating of behaviors you have witnessed.

The good news is that we aren't slaves to our genetics or the legacies left to us. We are new creations in Christ (2 Corinthians 5:17) and He can do a new work in not only us as individuals, but also our marriages when submitted to Him. 2 Corinthians 10:4 (NLT) says "We use God's mighty weapons, not worldly weapons, to knock down the strongholds of human reasoning and to destroy false arguments." Any lies we've grown up listening to, anything we've seen in our parents' marriages that were not healthy can be retaught. Our brains can literally grow new cells. This is a biblical concept that science is just catching up with in the last decade. Our brains are capable of changing. Our habits are capable of changing. But not in our own strength or wisdom! One of my all time favorite verses says "Don't copy the behavior and customs of this world, but let God transform you into a new person by changing the way you think. Then you will learn to know God's will for you, which is good and pleasing and perfect." Romans 12:2 (NLT)

We have a very fleshy, sinful nature from Christ. We aren't just going to magically change on our own. We need Jesus. We need His word. We can depend on Him to renew us, change us and help us overcome sin and character defects as we trust Him and obey Him. The Bible gives a blueprint for a healthy marriage and abundant life. There are so many sermons and biblically based books on marriage that can literally transform how you look at it and how you treat each other. There are biblical counselors who know what it takes to make a marriage go the distance. There are marriage based small groups in local churches. Feed yourself the truth. Equip yourself with the tools you need to see this thing survive. If you never go to church, only listen to secular music, watch toxic things on TV, hang around others whose lives aren't centered on Christ and think your life is headed anywhere good you're dead wrong. My mom always used to say garbage in, garbage out and I really believe that to be true. Give your body nutrient dense foods and watch it thrive. Feed it processed foods and chemicals and watch it become slowly poisoned. Same things with our mind. What are you reading? Watching? Listening to? Doing in your time off? Who do you hang out with? Is it the blind leading the blind or do you or your spouse have anyone to look up to, any sort of accountability? If you're reading this and thinking "uh oh," it's not too late! But it will require some effort on your part. Doing the same thing over and over expecting change is the definition of insanity. Turn your life and will over to the care of God. Trust and obey Him. Feed your mind with His goodness. Retrain it with His help. Don't be shy or ashamed. Get help! And prayer is one of the most powerful ways to do that.

Father, we come to You and ask You to expose any strongholds in our lives we aren't seeing. We ask You to expose any lies in our lives that we've been believing. We ask You to give us a hunger for Your word which exposes lies and replaces them with truth. We ask You for help. Lead us to the right verses, the right people, the right books, the right sermons, and the right churches and small groups so that we may be regularly fed the truth. Transform us Lord. We give You permission to come in and do what needs to be done in our hearts and minds and in our marriages. We pray we would tear down strongholds and stop repeating cycles that need to be broken. We can't do this alone. Please give us eyes to see our spouses through Your perspective. Please give us grace for them as we see they may be struggling with strongholds too. Teach us Lord to be good spouses. We can't do it alone. It's in the powerful name of Jesus Christ we pray. Amen.

EMAIL 25
VESSELS OF SANCTIFICATION

Before you get married, it's easy to hide the worst parts of yourself and put on a shiny mask because you know at some point, you can go home and let it all hang out. What's worse is that without someone around you all the time, you don't even see most of your sin because it isn't bothering you. It's when someone else is a victim of your bad behavior that you see it more clearly. Marriage exposes our flaws like nothing else can. There is no hiding when the mask comes off. Your spouse is there. All the time. So we are either forced to change or they are forced to adapt.

My friend Michelle made an interesting statement about this that has had me thinking: not only did God give her a husband with different strengths than her, He gave her a husband with flaws and sins that God intentionally uses to shape her and work out her own fears, flaws and sins. Their sin is our sanctification and vice versa. This thought has blown. My. MIND.

My sin, weaknesses and flaws are challenging, changing and sanctifying Dominic to be more Christ-like. His sin, weaknesses and flaws are doing the same to me. He actually joked early on in our marriage that I was his vessel of sanctification...lol!

I'm going to get a little personal with you here and give you a case in point: two of my biggest fears are financial insecurity and death. We grew up with a lot of financial ups and downs. This isn't a criticism of my parents because I know they did their absolute best! But I hated the roller coaster and as soon as I was old enough, I never had less than two or three jobs at a time until I started having children. I had those jobs out of fear. I didn't ever want to not have money. When I met Dominic he owned his own business. It's a cabinet/carpentry business where he remodels kitchens, bathrooms and garages and although he's very good at what he does, the construction business can be very inconsistent. God has put on both of our hearts for me to stay home with our children and although we are very certain and peaceful that we are walking in obedience, it brings up a lot of old fears in me! I'm not in control! I have to trust and depend on God to provide through my husband. It's something I have to constantly lay down at His feet which is definitely sanctifying and good, but so very hard!

My second fear doesn't need as much explanation as to where the root came from, but obviously since my first husband's sudden death, I find myself often fearful that the same thing could happen again. I was five months pregnant when Spencer died of an enlarged heart with ZERO symptoms. I honestly wanted to die right alongside of him. The thought that I could lose the love of my life suddenly and be devastated all over again leaves me paralyzed since I barely made it through that the first time. It doesn't help (or does it?) that God brought me a man who has really unhealthy habits! He smoked cigars daily when we first met (he doesn't now, praise God!), he drank sugary drinks and juices all day and he ate horribly and never exercised. He drinks water and eats much healthier now but these things made me face all those fears and realize once again, I'm not in control.

I actually asked God why, knowing my fears, that He couldn't have made him more healthy. I can't go into all the ways God made it obvious that Dominic was the man He had made for me because it would take too long, but He literally could not have made it more clear. And his health (or lack thereof) was intentional just like all the amazing things about him were intentional. It was to free me of these fears. You can't be free unless you face them and relinquish them to God. My lack of control over his body, his lifespan and his health forced me to my knees more times than I can count to acknowledge that God is sovereign, He is good and He loves me. Whatever happens, I can trust Him. If he had given me a marathon runner who juiced every morning or an accountant who had a predictable income, I would never have had to face these fears or remind myself of those truths. He is freeing me from bondage to fear in two really big areas that were hurting me in a way I couldn't see.

Your husband's strengths help you and shape you just like his weaknesses (and ours do the same for them!). This is not easy! But it does help us wriggle free from some chains in our lives. And it helps us not be so upset with them over the things that force us to see our own sin and fears because God is using them in our lives. The fact is we *are* married, for better or for worse, richer or poorer and in sickness and health and we are in a covenant with God, which means this is for the long haul. Rather than fight God (or our spouse) and get resentful at the things that are causing us discomfort, let's surrender that to Christ (maybe even thank Him for it?) and trust He will bring good out of it because His word promises that He will and He doesn't waste *anything* in our lives ("And we know that for those who love God all things work together for good, for those who are called according to his purpose." Romans 8:28).

Let's stop looking at our marriages to bring constant comfort and meet all our needs, and instead look at them as a classroom for Christ to teach us to be more like Himself: forgiving, not judging, loving unconditionally, and looking for ways to serve and bless rather than looking for ways to be served and blessed. There is such beauty in that kind of perspective change and it's one that takes practice, but it will forever change how we view our spouse, ourselves and our marriages…for the better.

Lord, help me and each one of these precious wives to see our husbands through Your eyes. Help us be quick to forgive, slow to judge or become angry, eager to love unconditionally and thoughtful to look for ways that we can serve and bless him. Let us be moldable in Your very trustworthy hands as you use our marriages to make us more like You. You are our heartbeat. Our Savior. Our rock, shield, redeemer and song. You are everything good and true. And we want You to shine through us by Your grace and the power of Your Holy Spirit. We love You Lord and we thank You for bringing our husbands into our lives. We lift them up to you and ask You to bless them and help them to become the men You want them to be. In Jesus' powerful and holy name, Amen.

EMAIL 26
LET'S TALK ABOUT SEX

Let's talk about sex! Again! Why? Because it's a vital part of our marriages. Also, it's a topic the world puts in our face daily, yet all too often the church remains eerily silent on the subject. Which is weird because God *created* sex. He designed it to be a beautiful and integral part of a marriage. However, the enemy has gotten a hold of it and twisted and perverted it into something it was never supposed to be. We can't turn our TV on without getting blasted by images or crude talk. There are billboards and magazines bombarding our minds and as a result, it's turned into something dirty instead of something meaningful. Instead of focusing on the negative parts, this is going to be a safe place where we can discuss how to have a healthy sex life with your husband.

First of all, there are many benefits to sex:
Spiritual Benefits (from the blog "To Love Honor and Vaccum"[1]):

> God created people with first and foremost a desperate longing for relationship.
> We long to know and be known, and in that spiritual knowing to be accepted.
> It's our deepest need. God gave us this drive to know Him and be known by Him, but He also gave us these sexual longings which mirror how we long to be truly united with our husbands and with God–to be truly and wonderfully KNOWN. Making love is supposed to be a true spiritual union–it's so much more than just having sex. Spiritual intimacy during sex ultimately depends on that desire to be united with your spouse. And that desire is fed throughout the day–by concentrating on what you love about him, by thinking about him, by flirting and playing with him, by saying positive things about him to others. It isn't something that "just happens". It's something that is the culmination of a relationship that you already have.

Emotional Benefits (from the blog "Very Well Mind"[2]) :

Increases level of commitment and helps spouses connect emotionally

Lowers feelings of insecurity and boosts self esteem

Helps with a more positive attitude, reduces irritability and increases sense of calm

Reduces depression and stress

Physical Benefits (from the blog "Very Well Mind"[2]):

Lowers the level of cortisol, a hormone that can trigger fatigue and cravings

Reduces pain by increasing endorphins

Vaginal tissue lubrication, improves pelvic muscle tone and prevents yeast infections

Lowers mortality rates and boosts libido

Reduced risk of prostate cancer and leads to better bladder control

Gives a youthful glow and increases circulation

Reduced risk of heart disease and lowers blood pressure

Helps people sleep better and improves memory

Improves immunity, digestion, sense of smell and memory

Produces chemicals in the brain to stimulate the growth of new dendrites

Sex often starts outside of the bedroom. A good marriage requires two servants. If you have two takers, it's a recipe for disaster. If you have one servant and one taker, it can be abusive. But two servants is the perfect recipe for intimacy inside and outside of the bedroom. Two questions to ask each other tonight might be: How can I better serve you outside of the bedroom? What about inside of the bedroom? It's good to be able to talk about this. It might be awkward if it's not something you're used to discussing, but it's important to keep the conversation open.

We have the unique privilege of being the one to satisfy our spouse sexually and mentally in a way no one else can. It's not something we ever want to use as weapon by either withholding as punishment or manipulation. There is a great video that talks about what men wish women knew and if you skip ahead to minute 22 it directly deals with the topic of sex: "**What Men Wish Women Knew**" with Priscilla Shirer (start at minute 22:24) https://youtu.be/VI17evdc02[3.] There is another video called *How to Have Good Sex in Marriage with Kay Arthur* (Start at minute 4:38) that will bless you too. You can access it here:http://www.lightsource.com/ministry/precepts/marriage-26-how-to-have-good-sex-in-marriage-469718.html

As our marriages progress, the sex should really get better with time and cultivating intimacy by talking about this with your spouse, praying about it together and guarding this precious gift will lead to that. Something you can start today is to prepare in advance for sex. Think about him throughout the day, send a sexy text, diffuse essential oils like ylang ylang, take a bath and shave your legs, get candles ready and start praying that the Lord would bless your evening and your intimacy.

Abba, please help us in this area You created. Help us to see it through Your eyes and not the distorted image of the world. I pray You would give us insight into our husband's needs and help us to love each other well in this way. Please keep our marriage pure from things that don't please You. Please keep it safe from adultery and pornography. I pray You would grow our desire for one another and unite us like never before physically, mentally and spiritually. May this be something we continue to bring to You in prayer and ask Your blessing and protection over. In Jesus' name we pray.

EMAIL 27
LETHAL SELF PITY

Over the last couple of years while doing marriage research for the *Warrior Wives Club*, three things have stood out to me that seem to lead to the slow deaths of marriages:

1. Focusing on the flaws of a spouse rather than the good.
2. Having unrealistic or un-communicated expectations.
3. Frequently giving in to self-pity.

Number three sounds dramatic and ominous, but I truly believe it's one of the main weapons Satan uses to build up resentment and bitterness in our hearts towards our spouse. Self-pity can lead to a hardness of heart *quickly* and at its root lies a spirit of pride, entitlement, and ungratefulness. The *Got Questions?* website gives some great insight:

> The biggest clue that self-pity is not of God is the word *self*. Any time we are focused on ourselves, other than for self-examination leading to repentance (1 Corinthians 11:28; 2 Corinthians 13:5), we are in the territory of the flesh. Our sinful flesh is the enemy of the Spirit (Romans 8:7). When we surrender our lives to Christ, our old nature is crucified with Him (Galatians 2:20; Romans 6:6). The *self*-ish, sinful part of our lives no longer needs to dominate. When Self is dominant, God is not. We, in effect, have become our own god. C. S. Lewis put it this way: "The moment you have a self at all, there is a possibility of putting yourself first—wanting to be the center—wanting to be God, in fact. That was the sin of Satan: and that was the sin he taught the human race."[1]

It's unbelievably easy to think of how we are being wronged, how we are misunderstood, how much we do that they don't see or help with, etc. Trust me, Satan is quick to feed you those lies when you are feeling tired or frustrated. Case in point: a few weeks ago I was loading up the boys and all of their stuff to take to my dad's so we could have a weekend away for our anniversary. Dominic had an appointment that morning with a client and as I was carrying down their things, all I could think was *This isn't how this was supposed to go! I'm pregnant and carrying heavy things out to the car by myself and I'm the only one who packed for them and....* Blah blah blah. It was ugly. As I was in the pit of self-pity, I started praying. I wanted this weekend to go well and it had already started with different expectations heading south so I was pretty sure the enemy was hard at work trying to ruin this thing. I started praying that I would calm down and see things clearly. God sure did answer me. He put on my heart that no one asked me to load the boys up by myself. I was the one who decided to go and do all of that instead of waiting an extra hour for Dom's help. He reminded me that if I had only asked, Dom would have been happy to help. In fact, when he found out later I had done all that by myself, he was upset with me that I didn't let him load the car and told me I needed to rest and be careful. I felt like a royal jerk! How could I have gotten it so wrong? It all started when I began entertaining those lies. We have a choice with our thoughts and I chose WRONG.

It got me wondering, is there ever a good reason to feel sorry for ourselves? I really can't think of one in light of Jesus and what He sacrificed for us. We have been saved from hell and have an eternity with Christ because of what He did for us on the cross. Anything good that comes our way beyond that is just overflow to a cup that is already full. And anything bad is not any worse than what we already deserved that Christ took for us.

Next time you start to feel sorry for yourself, take a moment and find a quiet spot to pray. My bathroom has become the ladder to climb out of my self-pity pit! No matter how justified I feel about being wronged or misunderstood or whatever lie the enemy is whispering to me, I try and go in there and dry up my tears or cool down my anger and pray that Jesus would replace whatever lie I'm believing with truth. I'm telling you: this *works*! I don't necessarily walk out of that bathroom a superhero within seconds of that prayer, but in a short amount of time, *every time*, this prayer is answered. The key is to really be willing to lay it down and let go of it, no matter how justified you feel. And if you don't feel like letting go of it, tell Him that too! Tell Him you need help to let go and that you want to want to surrender. It's incredible how you will have a new perspective about the situation in a short amount of time.

Father in Heaven, hallowed be Your name. Your kingdom come Your will be done on earth as it is in Heaven. I truly don't believe self-pity is ever a part of Your will. I pray You would help us recognize those thoughts and lies quickly, so we may confess them and take them captive and make them obedient to Jesus according to Your word in 1 Corinthians 10:5. If we are currently in that dark pit, we pray we would grab Your hand so that You can pull us out. Your word says in Psalm 40:2, "He lifted me out of the pit of despair, out of the mud and the mire. He set my feet on solid ground and steadied me as I walked along." May we walk on the solid ground of gratitude for our salvation and humility that we did nothing to deserve. May we be quick to forgive, quick to serve and most of all quick to love by the resurrection power that lies within us. In the name of our Lord and Savior Jesus Christ, we boldly ask these things. Amen.

EMAIL 28
FIGHTING FOR ONENESS

This week I'd like to address the topic of "oneness" which is definitely something I've dealt with over this past year and I thought maybe some of you could relate. I noticed that at the end of the week, I often feel disconnected from my husband. I've wondered why on Monday mornings I'm head over heels in love with my spouse, but by Friday I can often feel cold towards him. Am I struggling with some sort of mental illness here? Can I really be such a fickle pickle? What's going on?

For us personally, I think it has to do with leading two very different lives during the week. He runs his own business and deals with contractors, drawings and installations all day. I stay home with our babies and homeschool our oldest son. My conversations involve poop explosions and Trooper's science experiments while his involve the plumber who didn't show up or the screws he needs to buy to install his latest kitchen. DIFFERENT. We share a life but lead very different days. If we don't fight for oneness, fight to have those conversations at night about our days or take time to nurture one another during the week, by the time the week is over it feels like there is a lot of distance.

I say "fight" because those conversations don't necessarily come easy. If he is working late or we are both exhausted from our respective days, it's easy to turn over and go to bed in silence or zone out in front of the TV night after night. I'm not saying that that can never happen because let's be realistic: it will at times but we do need to fight for that connection more often than not. Weekends are great because you have more time together, therefore more opportunities to connect, but it can get lonely if you wait till then. And if you have busy weekends like we just had, you can run the risk of going not only days but possibly weeks without feeling "one."

Genesis 2:24 says: "Therefore a man shall leave his father and mother and hold fast to his wife and they shall become one flesh."

There are a lot of facets to being one besides the obvious physical oneness.

Marriage is the only relationship on earth where you experience intimacy on such an in-depth level. You truly become one in every sense. Becoming one means two complete people come together, complimenting each other to become better together than they could be on their own. We are better together than apart, but the culture we live in does not exactly promote "oneness." Busy-ness, self-sufficiency and independence are worn as badges of honor. Isolation from community, and even are own spouses, has become an epidemic with more and more "socializing" taking place with our phones and computers than with one another. Vacations are taken separately, bank accounts remain unjointed, bedtimes are never at the same time and separate hobbies begin to eat up free time. A couple I know who has been married almost 25 years just got divorced because they felt like "roommates." That didn't happen overnight. It happened with a lot of little, seemingly innocent choices.

This is a time to fight. The world does NOT have it right when it comes to keeping a strong marriage. Don't lead separate lives. Don't let your marriage grow cold. Don't give into the temptation of indifference. Learn to depend on one another and involve each other in your lives. Make time to reconnect by taking that relaxing bath together, having a weekly dinner for just the two of you, or having a "Monday Massage" night. Find hobbies together. Workout together. Play games together. Go to bed together. Go on adventures together. This is your one-flesh. Anything worth having is worth fighting for. And it wouldn't be a fight if that were effortlessly accomplished. We have to fight the proclivity of our flesh to go it alone. It's not easy but the reward is immense. There is nothing quite like the feeling of being loved and understood and "connected to" your spouse.

Lord, I pray You show us how to connect with our spouses tonight and this week. I pray You would not allow us to grow cold but to fight for oneness. I pray we would not look like the world. That we would not celebrate independence from our spouse but that we would learn to depend on one another, celebrate each other's victories, share in each other's hardships, and love each other well. This is hard, Lord. Marriage can be hard. But You made it. And as much as we want to fight for it, You want to fight for it more. You love marriage. You love OUR marriage. You love us. Please convict us in the areas where we might be dangerously vulnerable to independence from our spouse. Please give us the strength and wisdom to quickly correct that. In Your name we pray, Jesus, Amen.

EMAIL 29
THE PROBLEM OF PORN

This week's topic is a very serious one. It's one that hits close to home for me and my husband. In the years following my husband's death, I would find myself very drawn to movies or shows with sexual content. The desire I had was overwhelming at times and shows like "Sex and the City" or "Mad Men" or movies that might have nudity on Netflix were a huge temptation. I never ventured into anything online because I was afraid I might never turn back. When I met my husband, he confessed he had been single for four years since his last relationship and had struggled with internet pornography. It was something we both repented of to God and one another but the pull was still there. We ended up going to a group called "Recovery" once a week at our local church. It took us through the 12 steps with the Life Recovery Bible as our resource and thankfully the Lord has freed us from this.

I say all of this because it's important to recognize that both men and women can be addicted to pornography and it's a legitimate epidemic. We are bombarded with sexual images on our TV's, billboards, magazine racks, movies and computers. Sex is so beautiful and meaningful in the boundaries of marriage but what the Lord meant for good, Satan has twisted and perverted for evil. The enemy hates marriages and his goal is to alienate us from our spouses and to tear our families apart with divorce. Porn is one of his weapons and because it's absolutely everywhere, it's easy to justify, make jokes about or say that it's not a big deal because so many people struggle with it. But the fact is, it's very dangerous. It hurts our minds, it hurts our sex life, and it hurts our marriages.

The Pornography Epidemic Statistics (Clinton & Laaser):

There are 4.2 million pornographic websites.

There are 68 million pornographic search engine requests each day.

Porn revenue is larger than all combined reve03/24/19nues of all professional football, baseball, and basketball franchises.

Child pornography generates $3 billion annually.

40 million American adults regularly visit internet pornography websites.

53% of Promise Keepers men viewed pornography in the last week.

47% of Christians say pornography is a major problem in the home.

70% of women keep their cyber activities secret.

17% of all women struggle with pornography addiction.

The average age of first internet exposure to pornography is 11 years old.

90% of 8-16 year-olds have viewed pornography online (most while doing homework). [1]

As you can see from the statistics above, pornography is rampant in our society and a huge problem. Based on the statistics, there is a good chance that either you or your husband have struggled (or are struggling) with this. There is an amazing blog written by Kara Garis on the Desiring God website where she says "You and your husband together are in a battle against sin. Satan would love nothing more than to separate yet another covenant bond. Let me go ahead and affirm that, yes, an unfortunate consequence of sin is that it does hurt your relationship. Fight that with the blood of Christ. Forgiveness is offered to us all on the path back to marital unity. But in seeking "unity," we are not condoning sin. Be angry at the sin. Take note of Jesus and his anger — by grace, make it a righteous anger. "Be angry and do not sin" (Ephesians 4:26). Go to counseling. Pray together. Find a biblical community you can trust and be vulnerable with. Fight this sin together, and seek help from others. This fight together is not your doing or your undoing. Jesus is Lord over all, including your husband's struggles. Grace alone can bring about the permanent change your husband so desperately needs. Not you. You are not his Lord. You are not and have never been capable of changing someone else's heart condition. *If your husband will ever see the ugliness of porn, he must first see the beauty of Christ* as part of his daily experience of the Christian life. And you cannot give him such a spiritual vision. It is a gift from God." [2] [emphasis mine].

7 Steps to Overcome Pornography Use (Clinton & Laaser)[3]

Identify the Damage—evaluate how viewing pornography has been affecting your life, including obsessive thoughts that distract from more wholesome pursuits, distance in family relationships, and guilt.

Identify Patterns of Temptation—identify the locations and activities that provide temptation. Avoid stores that sell pornographic magazines. Use the computer only when someone else is in the room. Purchase software that blocks access to undesirable internet sites and become accountable to someone you trust.

Identify Emotional Triggers—are there work associates, times of the day, or particularly stressful situations that trigger the temptation? Take steps to minimize these triggers.

See It as Sin—it is important to see the behavior as sin and no longer justify it. Remember that even looking on someone lustfully is sinful, creating brokenness with God.

Refocus on Christ—develop a plan to strengthen and deepen your relationship with Jesus Christ. Be accountable to someone for daily Scripture reading and prayer. Memorize Scripture so that you can bring "every thought into captivity to the obedience of Christ" (2 Cor. 10:5).

Find Support and Accountability—become involved in a local Christian ministry that supports those who are experiencing this struggle.

See a Therapist Trained in Sexual Addiction Recovery— pornography use can lead to devastating, long-term problems, such as affairs, divorce, other forms of promiscuity, and sexually transmitted diseases. Find a professional who may help you recover from your pornography use and move forward with your life, free of the stronghold of porn.

If this has affected you or your marriage, there are things you can do. Prayer is always the best place to start and this is something we want to pray through with you. Hopefully, based on the information above and my own confession you will see this problem is widespread and you will not feel embarrassed or ashamed to reach out because chances are, you will be freeing others to do the same. You also want to get help from a recovery program or counselor. There are so many things, whether you are the one addicted or the one being hurt by the addiction, that need to be addressed such as shame, anger, fear, forgiveness, and broken trust. By facing this problem with God as your guide, the first steps toward healing can begin. You (and your marriage!) can end up stronger after the fact because that's how amazing our God is. We are a testAment to this.

Resources:
My in-laws have a marriage ministry called "Married For Life." It's a great marriage class that can be done online with another married couple or group of married couples to strengthen your marriage. However, if someone comes to them and has a pornography problem, they send them to a different ministry to seek help overcoming that addiction and once that is dealt with, they encourage them to come back and rebuild their foundation and trust with Married for Life.

The two resources they suggest are Pure Desire (https://www.puredesire.org/) and Faithful and True (https://www.faithfulandtrue.com/)

It is strongly recommended that the person who is caught in this addiction seek counseling and get an accountability partner and join an accountability group. There are Sexual Addiction groups in almost every city.

Local churches can often guide you in this and sometimes have meetings themselves. One of my favorite churches in our area is called Summit Church. On Thursday nights, they have a group called "Recovery" that I mentioned before and they are an excellent place to seek help. http://www.recoveryatsummit.com/ If you know this is an issue in your home or you want to be preventative, there are some anti-porn softwares you can install

on your devices. Two that I did a bit of research on are:
www.covenanteyes.com and https://x3watch.com/

Focus on the family recommends a book called *5 Steps to Breaking Free From Porn* by Joe Dallas that you can purchase here: https://store.focusonthefamily.com/5-steps-to-breaking-free-from-porn?visitorid=4b11d6ae-dfa8-4162-b9cc-4ccfa4223195&extra_data=%7B%7D&_ga=2.214906007.1812128998.1529085035-1143620173.1529085035

Father, my heart is heavy thinking about the women who right at this moment are raw and hurting, feeling betrayed by this. I pray You would remind them they aren't alone and that You can and will help them. My heart is also heavy for those who have struggled with this sin and the shame that they feel. Lord, I ask that You would do a mighty work in our marriages. Please give us eyes only for one another. Help us be a "one man" woman and our husbands to be a "one woman" man. We pray for freedom from the enemy's lies that true sexual satisfaction can be found outside the beautiful boundaries You gave us in marriage. I pray for healing over hurt minds and hearts because You are the only One who can truly do that. Forgive us Lord in the areas we've compromised and restore to us the purity that comes from being forgiven and washed in the blood of the Lamb. It's in His powerful name, the Name above all names, Jesus Christ that we pray for Your help. Amen.

EMAIL 30
ARE YOU SMARTER THAN YOUR HUSBAND?

I think if we are all honest with ourselves, at some point in our marriage we have thought this: "Why won't he just listen to me?" Or "What a bad decision! I can't believe he did that!" or some variation of the sort.

We might not have actually thought or said the words "I'm smarter than him," but in our heart of hearts, we have believed that at some point. The reason I'm going out on a limb here and lumping us all in this together is that the women that I am most transparent with in my life have admitted to sharing these feelings. And after some further research, I realize this might actually be an epidemic!

It's not pretty. It's not admirable. But did you know it's biblical? Bear with me for a minute...

"To the woman he said, "I will surely multiply your pain in childbearing; in pain you shall bring forth children. Your desire shall be for your husband, and he shall rule over you" (Genesis 3:16).

In the NLT version the translation says, "Then he said to the woman, 'I will sharpen the pain of your pregnancy, and in pain you will give birth. And you will desire to control your husband, but he will rule over you.'"

Hence began the power struggle we all face in our marriages at some point or another. Our natural proclivity towards sin in our different genders is for men to want to work all the time (Genesis 3:17) and for women to want to rule over her husband. Control can lead to a decrease in our intimacy and can come in some really ugly packages such as manipulation in order to get what we want.

In so many ways, God has given us beautiful differences as men and women. Unfortunately in our current culture, we tend not to celebrate these differences but try and control others due to their differences. And cultural or not, I believe the timeless struggle for us as women is to fight the prideful thought that we think we are smarter than our husbands and to try and control them as a result. The fact of the matter is, in some ways we are smarter! But our pride tends to take over and instead of realizing that in some ways they are smarter than us as well, we run with those thoughts and judgments and condescending words. Or we tend to let spew out of us.

We all have certain gifts. And we *are* different, which is why marriage is such a beautiful thing. We need each other to be complete. We each bring something unique to the table that the other can't and that is such a gift if only we could receive it and see the benefit.

I heard Rick Warren say on Moody Radio that the Lord talks about "two character traits that lead to His presence, His peace, His power and His blessing: generosity and humility."[1] He also said in his book *Purpose Driven Life* that "being humble is not thinking less of yourself; it is thinking of yourself less."[2] The best relationships in marriage and in friendship have humility as a foundation. If we could take ourselves off the front burner for a bit, we would actually experience freedom and joy in a way self-focus does not allow.

There will be times where he makes the wrong decision but heck! There will be times when we do too. Sometimes we think we know what is best and try to control the situation accordingly. However, what we *think* is best may not be and it's important to lay down our pride and consider their perspective because they are making decisions with the knowledge they have just like we do. When it's the wrong one, we should show grace the same way we would hope they would show us grace if the situation were reversed and the same way we have been shown grace by our Heavenly Father. In the article *Why Controlling Women Kill Relationships* Dr. Julie

Stratus says, "You can let go of control when you truly grasp this: the most effective thing you can do to influence those you love is to pray for them and demonstrate a genuine trust in God's work in your own life. Chances are that the most influential people in your life did exactly that. They never forced or manipulated you into decisions but encouraged, loved, and modeled the behaviors they believed in."[3]

At the end of the day, our husbands want to feel respected above all else; even more than loved! (Ephesians 5:22-33). This week if/when those feelings of wanting to be in control or rule over your hubby starts to cloud your mind, take a moment and pray that God would allow you to see your spouse through His eyes and give you the grace to trust Christ in him and in yourself. Ask Him to show you how to love and respect your husband the way he needs and longs for and to truly let go of any desire to control or manipulate. And maybe even ask for a dose of humility if you dare! That one gets me every time!

Lord, we humbly confess and repent of the times we have proudly thought we were smarter than our husbands out of a desire to control them. We ask Your forgiveness for times we have tried use manipulation to get our own way. We pray You would help us die to this sin bent within us, because it is no longer we who live but Christ who lives in us (Galatians 2:20). Please give us the grace to respect and love our husbands the way You desire for us to. Please remind us to be humble and to think of ourselves less. We trust You are working in them and in us and in those moments we forget that, we ask for the grace to trust You more. You are so worthy and we would ruin things if we were in control. We thank You that You are sovereign and that we are not. We give YOU the control of our lives and our marriages. It's only in Your hands that we are safe. It's in Jesus' name that we pray, Amen.

EMAIL 31
REVERSE LOVE LANGUAGES

Most of us have heard of the *Five Love Languages* written by Gary Chapman. I think it's a brilliant book that can help you better understand how you, your spouse, your children and others in your life both give and receive love. It was pretty mind blowing for me when I realized my oldest son would become a different person with just a little quality time playing Legos or how my middle son would immediately calm down with a hug or reading to him while he sat in my lap. If you aren't familiar with the book, I highly recommend reading it, but the gist is that Dr. Chapman has noticed patterns in the way partners communicate. If we can figure those out, we can see what their unvoiced expectations are and meet those needs. The five ways most people give or receive love are[1]:

1. **Words of Affirmation**
2. **Quality Time**
3. **Receiving Gifts**
4. **Acts of Service**
5. **Physical Touch**

When we figure out what our spouse needs, then we need to make sure to show them love in that way. I totally agree with this, but a counselor shared with me once that there is a way we could take this to the next level where it is sustainable. Let me explain. If a wife feels most loved with a love letter or some other declaration but this isn't her husband's gift, she will spend the majority of her marriage frustrated. Sure she can tell him what she needs and he can muster up enough courage to go outside of his comfort zone. That might last a couple months or he might make sure to do that on an anniversary in a special way since that's what is important to her. But what about all the other days where he is showing her love in the way that is most natural to him? In a way that organically overflows from how he feels?

For example, I'm a words of affirmation girl for sure. If Dom wrote me a flowery email or went on and on about all the ways he loved me, I would melt. But he is a man of few words and because he's French, reading and writing in English can be really exhausting and painstaking for him. Knowing this about me, he definitely tries! But his daily, natural overflow of showing love is acts of service. Knowing that, I now look for those times and make a conscious note in my head to "receive" love when he is showing it to me. When he gets up with the kids most mornings and lets me sleep an extra hour, he is showing me love (who knew "sleep" was my new love language?!). If he does the dishes (which I know for a fact he hates by the way), I remind myself, *Hey, Lady! He is loving you hard right now!*

Sometimes out of nowhere he will tell me how much he really loves me or that he thinks I'm a rock star wife and mom. One time he said he never knew he could love someone as much as he loves me. You know what I did? I wrote it down! I literally keep a note in my phone for the sweet things he says and that way if I'm needing a bit of affirmation or doubting how he feels, it's there and I'm not nagging him to produce something for me just because I'm feeling insecure. This doesn't mean you shouldn't let them know how you are wired or that you should shrug off their need for a certain love language just because it doesn't come easily to you! Dom loves physical touch. He is always holding my hand and wanting to snuggle at night, but after a long day with three boys, this is not my favorite thing to do. But sometimes I will come out from my mound of pillows and make it a point to lay my head on his chest because I know he loves it (until he falls asleep anyway, then I sneak back to my pillow mountain like the ninja that I am).

It's important to know how your spouse gives and receives love and it's important they understand you as well. I can't recommend Dr. Chapman's book enough for that reason. But the key is to get your "love tank"[2] filled by God first and then everything else is just icing. It actually makes for a much more peaceful marriage to understand God made your spouse a certain way and you can't change them, nor should you. You can pray for God to show you that assurance, but in my experience, if I'm feeling unloved it is usually an indicator of my time (or lack of time) with the Lord. When I'm truly satisfied in Him and aware of His love for me, I am full to the point where I can overflow that love onto my spouse, my children and others. And when they show me their love, I'm not desperately taking it in like a dry desert in need of rain. I can receive it with a grateful heart and a smile knowing I'm fully loved by my Creator and in His infinite grace, He gave me a little tribe to love on and to be loved on by them, and that He created them to show love in their own different ways. It's one of the greatest blessings of my life, but being full of His love doesn't put me in a place to be dependent on their love, it puts me in a place where I can water them with His.

Lord, thank You for making us all so uniquely and wonderfully. Thank You for all the ways You show us love and that You have wired us to show love to one another. We pray You would make us hypersensitive to the ways our husbands need to be loved and that You would love them through us. We also pray You would make us hypersensitive to how they are showing us love, even if it's not the way we would necessarily prefer. We pray You would soften our hearts to one another, allowing us to first be full of Your love and second to extend that love to one another. We love because You first loved us and for that we are eternally grateful. In the powerful name of Jesus, the One who gave up His life for us so that we might find ours, Amen.

EMAIL 32
IN SICKNESS AND IN HEALTH

This year I've gotten a new perspective on the part of our vows "in sickness and in health." Truth be told, I always thought I would be a great wife in that situation. I actually really love to serve others and although I hoped with all my heart my spouse would never be sick, I just assumed if it did happen, I would be able to handle it with grace.

I got the *tiniest* peak of what that might look like and what I saw was not what I imagined. Dominic came home from a long day of work one evening with a backache. That night, he couldn't even walk to bed. The next day was even worse. He couldn't even get to the bathroom on his own. He was flat on his back for two weeks and unable to do much more than sit for short periods for four weeks after that. We'd been to the chiropractor and a therapeutic massage therapist and he got much better, but for a busy guy who rarely sits down, this was quite a shock to both of us.

Please don't misunderstand me and think I'm comparing a thrown-out back to a spouse who is caring for someone who is chronically ill or disabled or dealing with cancer. I'm just saying that those six weeks gave me a brand new empathy for those who are in the situation of having a sick spouse. Here are the things that were surprising to me:

1. You feel helpless. It's unbelievably horrible to watch your favorite person in excruciating pain. Not knowing how to help is a scary feeling. You feel lonely. Not only is it difficult watching them be in pain, but because of that pain they aren't themselves and you miss them.

2. You're exhausted. You have to wait on them for every need on top of your normal responsibilities *in addition* to taking on the things they are normally responsible for. It's overwhelming and you don't want to make them feel even worse by showing them you're tired and overwhelmed so you put on a happy face, but that takes extra energy too!

3. There is probably a financial aspect that you are now dealing with. For us almost two months of not working was really difficult budget-wise. I can't imagine someone who has to deal with the loss of an income for an extended period of time on top of medical expenses.

4. Fear of the unknown. What if they don't get better? What if this is your life now? I'm so thankful he's back to normal now but the thought did cross my mind before we were able to get him there, "What if this is permanent? What will that mean for our family?"

I think when we say these vows, we don't realize how hard it will be if/when that time comes around. The word **vow** by definition in verb form is to "solemnly promise to do a specified thing." [1] When we stand in front of each other we say the *noun* part and make the solemn promise. But in marriage when that promise is actually put into play, the vow becomes a verb and we walk that promise out. It's important to promise beforehand so you can remind yourself of it and that a promise is not kept or broken based on how you feel. It's kept because you made that promise before God to one another and that means something.

Again, please don't think me overly dramatic because I was in no way questioning my vows these last few months! But my point is that after only a few *days*, I was tired. He was tired. It wasn't easy. And after several weeks we were at the end of ourselves. Like I said previously, I imagined myself handling this with grace. Picture an angelic wife floating to her husband's bedside with a warm smile, a kiss on his cheek and encouraging words. What actually went down was me rushing in to help him with a baby on my hip, a toddler throwing a tantrum in the hallway, dinner burning, sweat dripping down my face and a tightening in my throat from fighting back tears. I felt stretched and panicked and I just wanted him to get back to normal so I wasn't doing everything on my own. Nice, huh? Definitely not how I thought I would be. But I'm glad! That was real life! I have a deeper compassion for our bookkeeper whose husband is fighting cancer. He is on a feeding tube and all the appointments she has to take him to and the new life they are facing has to be overwhelming to say the least. I called her to tell her I will be praying even more for her than I already was and that I thought she was a saint. Dom told her that he had an incredible new amount of compassion for her husband who is so sickly he is in a wheelchair and can't walk or eat on his own. Dom's heart broke for how helpless he must feel because for a man to feel useless, it's devastating.

God brings good out of everything for those who love Him (Romans 8:28) and the good that came from these past couple of months were more compassion for those who are sick and hurting and for those who are *helping* those who are sick and hurting. It gave us new perspective on the promises made in our marriage. When Dom told me one night that he felt bad because of how I was serving him non-stop, I told him that I *knew* if the situation were reversed, he would do the same for me and this was part of the deal: in sickness and in health. He smiled and squeezed my hand because we both know we aren't going anywhere, no matter how hard it gets. This has made us stronger.

I know of another woman whose husband is fighting liver failure and two other marriages where mental illness is a prevalent issue. I'm sure you know others in your own lives who are in a similar situation. My challenge to us this week is to say an extra prayer for these couples. And if you have time, maybe call, make a meal, or send a letter of encouragement. It will mean a great deal to them.

Lord, by Your strength, and Your strength alone, we will walk out these vows till the end and leave a legacy to those around us and bring glory to You who made us. Thank You for the gift of marriage. Thank You that you give us everything we need to love and serve our spouse. It's in the name of Jesus we pray that we would be a vessel of kindness and encouragement to them. Amen.

EMAIL 33
ARE YOU PROTECTING YOURSELF?

Stop trying to protect yourself, and be all in.

Our culture doesn't always make it easy to stay married, does it? One of the messages we hear is that we should keep a little piece of ourselves private. You know, like feelings you keep from your spouse but share with some other friend, a secret bank account with a little stash on the side "just in case," or whatever your back-up plan is should he leave or die.

The world tells us these are wise things to do. Yet the actions we take to protect ourselves actually build a wall. They create a lack of trust. They cause suspicion to creep in. In other words, they create the very problem we are trying to protect ourselves from.

God has designed marriage to be the ultimate "all in" institution. That is why God joins a man and a woman for life. He wants us to be set free to take what seems like the scary risk of complete, naked, utter transparency with no self-protection, knowing that the other person isn't going anywhere. It can indeed feel scary to step out in that way. But once we do, we find that this ultimate risk is what creates the ultimate security. The root of us protecting ourselves can often be traced back to us not trusting the Lord as our Ultimate Protector. Psalm 121:5 (NLT) says "The Lord himself watches over you! The Lord stands beside you as your protective shade."

In my own life and in the lives of my friends, the couples who are all in move from being very troubled in their marriage to being very happy. And the change comes when they stopped trying to protect themselves and eliminated their other options. They literally removed the word "divorce" from their vocabularies. They took a deep breath and gave each other full access to parts of their lives they had previously kept private. They made themselves completely vulnerable to each other, even at the risk of being hurt through unforeseen death or tragedy.

Is there something you're holding back? If you're afraid of the "what if," find boldness in God's great love for you. Proverbs 3:5-6 says to "Trust in the LORD with all your heart and lean not on your own understanding; in all your ways submit to him, and he will make your paths straight." Don't lean on your own understanding because your perspective may be clouded by hurt feelings and suspicions. Instead, trust Him. Let His love come in and banish the fear that causes you to hold back in your marriage. In scripture, we are told not to fear over 100 times. He is serious about this! And in most instances it is followed by the promise that He is with us. When you believe God and stand on His promises, you can confidently let go of the fears that divide you from your spouse, "for God gave us a spirit not of fear but of power and love and self-control." 2 Timothy 1:7. In marriage, you truly get what you give. We get so much more when we give our spouses our all. So go ahead: jump into the deep end and get in over your head! You will find God is there with you every inch of the way.

Dear Lord, if there are any areas of my life I have withheld from my spouse, help me to let go of the fears and mistrust that have caused me to do that. I choose to set aside my own understanding, and let Your love fill my heart so I can be confident in You. Give me wisdom as I open up to my spouse so that we can be unified together in our marriage. I trust in You as my protector, knowing with You being for me, no back up plan is needed. Amen.

EMAIL 34
CHECK YOUR BEARINGS

I'm so thankful to be on this journey with you, praying through so many different things together and praising God for so many amazing victories. What a beautiful privilege this has been! I pray for another year of standing together for our marriages, refusing to let the enemy have a foothold in the most important human relationship we will have on this earth.

As we enter the new year, one of my favorite pastors says it's a great time to "check your bearings because sometimes you can be making great time, but heading in the wrong direction." Last night Dom and I were able to go on a date and we got to talk about some things we'd like to do differently this year. Some things we wanted to leave behind and some things we wanted to work on or add in. My challenge to each of you (and to me!) is to not only have that conversation with your husband but also really take the time to go before the Lord together. We make lists, we spend time worrying about this or that, but so much more would be accomplished in prayer. I thought about that after we left dinner. It's one thing to talk about it, but if we really want to see a change, we need to pray about it and invite our Heavenly Father into every area of our lives.

Something I'm wanting to ask the Lord both individually and together is what **He** would like us to cut out and if there is anything we need to be doing that we aren't. What we want and what the Lord wants could be totally different and I don't want us to waste our time doing things in the flesh (which leads to death) and not the Spirit (which leads to life). Romans 8:6 (NLT) says, "For to set the mind on the flesh is death, but to set the mind on the Spirit is life and peace." The world is LOUD and is going to tell us what our priorities should be. And it's going to appeal to our flesh! But do you know what? Those priorities are going to be in direct conflict with scripture. Jesus says in John 17:16 that "They are not of the world, just as I am not of the world."

We are here but we are not from here and we are *supposed* to look different. We are citizens of a different kingdom. Citizens of Heaven! Daughters of the Most High God. We should NOT look like everyone else. Our priorities should be different. The world is going to tell you your happiness or your career or your popularity is more important than your marriage and your relationships. The world is going to tell you making money and making your house perfect and your body perfect should be what we spend our time and resources on, but all of these things are quite literally wasting away. They are temporary. It makes zero sense to give *so much* of our energy to things that won't matter in 50 years. Seriously and honestly write down what you spend the most money and time on and that will show you where your priorities are. I don't think there is one among us who couldn't use a little tweaking in this area. I strongly believe if we have a long list of resolutions we could cross them all off and just write: Spend more time with Jesus asking Him for *His* agenda, not my own. Spend more time with my husband (and kids if you have them). Spend more time loving and serving others. These three things encompass so much and would make for one beautiful year if they were truly what we focused on.

When someone asked Jesus what the greatest commands are He replied: ""You shall love the Lord your God with all your heart and with all your soul and with all your mind. This is the great and first commandment. And a second is like it: You shall love your neighbor as yourself. On these two commandments depend all the Law and the Prophets." (Matthew 22:36-40). They *hang* on these two commandments. If we resolved to prioritize these two things, we wouldn't have to worry about any of the other ones because if you are loving the Lord and others, then things like adultery, murder (which can be as simple as contempt for someone else),and coveting (that's comparison too! Anyone else look at instagram and think I wish I were on that vacation or wow that family seems totally perfect?), would not be a problem. When you have Jesus, you have everything. You treat others differently (yourself included!) because you know you are truly and unconditionally loved and your identity is in Him.

Are you heading down the right path? You might think you are, but if not He will show You and wants to redirect you down the path of life everlasting. Or maybe you know you aren't but you aren't sure how to get back. Just stop! Take a breath. Pray. Ask Him to turn you around. (Proverbs 4:25-27 says, "Let your eyes look straight ahead; fix your gaze directly before you. Give careful thought to the paths for your feet and be steadfast in all your ways. Do not turn to the right or the left; keep your foot from evil.") And don't run ahead but stay in step with Him, being dependent moment by moment, day by day. Deuteronomy 5:32 says, "You shall be careful therefore to do as the LORD your God has commanded you. You shall not turn aside to the right hand or to the left." Don't make one more decision without consulting the Sovereign God who made you and knows you and knows what is coming in your future. He is your Abba. Your Daddy. He wants what is best for you and WANTS to guide you. So let Him! It may look totally different than what you would have thought (in fact I promise you it will!), but focusing on Him and letting Him direct your steps will lead to true joy and peace because He always has your good in mind.

Father, Your Word says in Isaiah 30:21, "And your ears shall hear a word behind you, saying, "This is the way, walk in it," when you turn to the right or when you turn to the left." We pray You would give us ears to hear You. It also says in Proverbs 3:5-6 to "Trust in the Lord with all your heart, and do not lean on your own understanding. In all your ways acknowledge Him, and He will make straight your paths." We trust You, Abba. We ask You to make our paths straight and align our dreams, desires and agendas with You. We want to put You and Your kingdom first because everything else is temporary. We thank You for the privilege of getting to walk with You and being called Your child and we thank You that through Jesus that is possible. It's in His perfect and righteous name we pray, Amen.

EMAIL 35
CHECK YOUR BLINDSPOT

Last week we talked about checking our bearings and asked the Lord to show us if we are heading in the direction He would have for us. Our meeting on Wednesday was a powerful one where we were able to watch a clip of *War Room* and then had time to discuss and pray for our marriages. I don't know if there was a dry eye in the place! If you haven't seen *War Room*, rent it tonight. Or soon at least! Ha. I've seen it two or three times now but I'm always *so inspired* by how the Lord can change hearts through the power of prayer. Every time I see it I am reminded that no situation is hopeless if placed in the hands of our Mighty God.

This week I would like to challenge you to check your blindspot. In three separate but consecutive conversations I've recently had with others, the person was describing a problem in their life but it's as if they were totally oblivious to the root of that problem. They had a huge blindspot. I came home after one such conversation and asked Dominic, "Where's *my* blindspot?!" I am not naive enough to think that if these highly intelligent and lovely people could be so unaware of a big issue that was wreaking havoc in their lives that I might not have one (or more!) of my own. I genuinely asked Dom if he could see something I was ignoring or unaware of, but he said he couldn't think of one (maybe my pregnancy and the emotional roller coaster I've been on lately have him treading lightly). I really wanted to know though so who better to ask about the hidden places of my heart than the One who created me? David's prayer seemed perfect for this request in Psalm 139:23-24 (NLT): "Search me, God, and know my heart; test me and know my anxious thoughts. Point out anything in me that offends You, and lead me along the path of everlasting life."

Let me just tell you, that's not exactly a fun prayer to have answered but it sure is a freeing one. The Lord definitely exposed some sin areas in my life I needed to deal with but you know what? He doesn't wag His finger at us and say, "Now go ahead. Work on those and I'll check back with you in a few weeks to see how you're doing." Nope. He shows us our sin in His mercy so we can repent of it and receive the *immediate* forgiveness Christ died to give us. 1 John 1:19 says, "If we confess our sins, he is faithful and just to forgive us our sins and to cleanse us from all unrighteousness." Colossians 1:13-14 says, "He has delivered us from the domain of darkness and transferred us to the kingdom of his beloved Son, in whom we have redemption, the forgiveness of sins."

In addition, He gives us the strength to avoid those sins in the future: "The temptations in your life are no different from what others experience. And God is faithful. He will not allow the temptation to be more than you can stand. When you are tempted, he will show you a way out so that you can endure" 1 Corinthians 10:13 (NLT). Then He genuinely changes us (sometimes immediately and sometimes over time) to where we think differently and don't struggle in those areas any more: "This means that anyone who belongs to Christ has become a new person. The old life is gone; a new life has begun!" 2 Corinthians 5:17 (NLT).

I would challenge you this week to ask the Lord if there are any blindspots in your life. As He shows you, ask His forgiveness and then immediately thank Him for it. The second step is really important according to Francis Schaeffer in his book *The Finished Work of Christ*, because it brings us into agreement with what is already true. He writes, "Having admitted your sin and having brought it under the blood of Christ, say thank you. And I think you'll immediately find that, as soon as you say thank you, the certainty of your forgiveness will come and you will have peace of mind."[1]

In regard to our marriages, I think it's important to regularly ask the Lord to expose sin in our lives. For one thing, it keeps us humble. It's very easy to notice all the things wrong with the person you are around the most and when we ask the Lord to help us see our own wrongs, it takes the heat off of them and it helps us appreciate our husband more for being with us despite all our own shortcomings. It creates feelings of gratitude, empathy and understanding instead of judgment, anger and bitterness. If the Lord shows you a sin that has been affecting your spouse, confessing it to them and asking their forgiveness does WONDERS for a relationship. It kicks Satan in the teeth with any ground he might be trying to gain by dividing you. And again it shows humility and can create a safe space for your spouse to do the same. A marriage where forgiveness is asked for frequently is a marriage that is prepared for for the long haul. Two sinful beings WILL hurt each other so it's only natural that we would seek their forgiveness and then give it freely when asked: "Be kind to one another, tenderhearted, forgiving one another, as God in Christ forgave you," Ephesians 4:32).

The War Room movie inspired me to finally start my own prayer closet. It's not a closet per say because our baby currently sleeps in our closet (#truestory) but more of an area of the wall next to my bed. To be honest, I really didn't think writing down some prayers and taping them up would really help all that much. But man it sure worked in the movie which is based on a scripture so I thought I'd give it a go. Here's what I learned: it totally works. I'm so serious! First of all, it helped me mentally to write things down and stay focused. Second, it put my mind in the practice of prayer and I have found that I've been praying almost constantly throughout the day since starting this. Third, it helped me get outside of my own issues because as I sat there with the sole purpose of praying, the Lord would put people in my mind and I would pray for others I might normally not have taken the time to. Fourth, every time I walk by that wall, I'm reminded He's at work and I'm waiting expectantly and excitedly to see what He does. It will be awesome and faith-building to see these things answered that normally, had I not written them down, I might have forgotten about otherwise. All that to say, maybe start a prayer closet (or wall!) this week and start praying about your blindspot! He is faithful to expose and forgive the sins in our lives.

Father, I thank You that because of Your son our sin is paid for. I thank You that the moment we ask, You forgive us and that You help us to not stay in our sin but rather, You change our hearts and minds and give us a distaste for it. We ask as wives to have our sin exposed, for courage to confess it to You and our spouse, and for humility because that is an attribute that is so beautiful and representative of Christ. It's in His precious and life-saving name that we pray, Amen.

EMAIL 36
HOW TO SUBMIT

The word submission has such a bad connotation and has veered heavily in our culture from the beauty of its meaning in scripture. Growing up with a grandmother who was abused by her stepdad and then her husband, that word not only brought up fear in my heart but also anger. I never wanted to be in a position where I could be hurt and feel like I had no way out so I was a feminist through and through for years. I never wanted to get married. I went to school to get a minor in Spanish, a bachelors in marketing and then a masters in international business because I was never going to put myself in a situation where I had to depend on a man.

Skip ahead a few years and I truly gave my life to Christ and He changed my idea about how marriage was supposed to look. He showed me that submitting to your husband was actually submitting to Him if your husband has Christ in his heart and that it was supposed to be a beautiful hedge of protection for me. I actually really loved this description:

> "Submit is not a bad word. Submission is not a reflection of inferiority or lesser worth. Christ constantly submitted Himself to the will of the Father (Luke 22:42; John 5:30), without giving up an iota of His worth. To counter the world's misinformation concerning a wife's submission to her husband, we should carefully note the following in Ephesians 5:22–24: 1) A wife is to submit to one man (her husband), not to every man. The rule to submit does not extend to a woman's place in society at large. 2) A wife is to willingly submit to her husband in personal obedience to the Lord Jesus. She submits to her husband because she loves Jesus. 3) The example of a wife's submission is that of the church to Christ. 4) There is nothing said of the wife's abilities, talents, or worth; the fact that she submits to her own husband does not imply that she is inferior or less worthy in any way. Also notice

that there are no qualifiers to the command to submit, except "in everything." So, the husband does not have to pass an aptitude test or an intelligence test before his wife submits. It may be a fact that she is better qualified than he to lead in many ways, but she chooses to follow the Lord's instruction by submitting to her husband's leadership. In so doing, a godly wife can even win her unbelieving husband to the Lord "without words" simply by her holy behavior (1 Peter 3:1).[1]

Our God is a God of order and peace not confusion and chaos. I truly believe when we follow scripture, our lives work how they are supposed to. I've seen too many marriages where there were two captains of the ship and the ship went down because each was trying to assert their authority. I've also seen situations where the wife is "the boss" and controls every detail of their lives and it truly emasculates the husband over time and sets a horrible example for their children. Now, I'm sure you've wondered as I have about submission if there is abuse present or if the husband isn't following the Lord. If there is abuse, you have a responsibility to yourself and your children to protect yourself. You are not supposed to submit where you are physically in danger! And if your husband is asking you to do something that goes against scripture, our first responsibility is to obey the Lord and not use one scripture out of context as an excuse to sin or not take responsibility for our actions. However, in my experience of witnessing different marriages, this is truly the exception to the rule. What I've seen more commonly is a fear of submitting when we don't agree with something they are about to do or a deep sense of pride believing our way is the right way and insisting upon it.

So what happens when we don't agree? I don't think there is one among us who can honestly say they have agreed with *everything* their husband has said or done (on that note I'm sure there isn't a husband in this group who could say the same about us!). Some of you might be in this exact place right now. Or maybe you've been there before. You're afraid his bad choice is going to hurt you or your family. But did you know there is protection for you despite his behavior? Another dear friend shared a story with me a long time ago that has stuck with me. She came to know Christ about ten years before her husband did. She read in the word about submitting to her husband, but with her husband not being a believer or acting according to the word of God, this required a lot of trust in the Lord on her part. She said time and time again she would see the Lord act on her behalf even if she didn't agree with what her husband was doing. But she believed the Bible and knew He was faithful to His word and she saw him bless her over and over again and bring good out of things despite his decisions. Ten years later he came to know the Lord himself. One of the things that brought him to the Lord was the way his wife conducted herself. He saw the change in her from being overbearing and mean (prior to being saved by Christ) to being loving, kind and respectful. Her behavior towards him, her prayers on behalf of him and her trust in Jesus quite literally "won him over" like the verse above describes.

When we are in a situation where there is a standoff and we are fighting our flesh to submit and insisting on our own way, I would encourage you to pray that the Lord's will be done through your husband. He is worthy of our trust and He is more than capable of changing the will of our husband to line up with His perfect one. We do not need to fear the outcome of our husband's choices. We only need to be faithful to the word of God. He can bring good out of *anything* for those who love Him (Romans 8:28). I leave you with this verse: "But you, O Lord, are a shield around me; you are my glory, the one who holds my head high. I cried out to the Lord, and he answered me from his holy mountain" (Psalm 3:3-4, NLT).

Lord, You alone are our shield no matter what we face. You hold our head high. I pray these verses bless us and take root in our heart and that by Your grace, our holy beauty would impact our husbands in an unprecedented way. We pray for freedom from fear because that is not a spirit You give us. Your word says in 2 Timothy 1:7 that You give us a spirit of love, power and self-control, so we receive that gift and thank You for it. In Jesus' name, Amen.

EMAIL 37
LIES WE BELIEVE:
TRUTH VERSES FEELINGS

Ok, this one will be hard to write because it's very personal and honestly it's still a bit raw.

For two days I was absolutely furious at Dominic. By the way, nothing had happened. I'd love to claim pregnancy hormones here and I'm sure that might be a part of it, but honestly, it felt darker than that. I finally realized I was really being spiritually attacked. How did I know that? Well, often you don't recognize it right away. You have thoughts in your head that can make you feel a certain way towards a person out of nowhere. If you entertain them and don't bring them into alignment with what God says in His Word pretty quickly, those thoughts can become full-out feelings. I saw this meme on instagram over the weekend that says, "The devil wants you to pay attention to your feelings, Jesus wants you to pay attention to His truth." That is so right on. You can feel a certain way that is based on absolutely zero truth but if you don't speak out what is making you believe that thought, it can get bigger, darker, scarier, and angrier.

One example that always reminds me of this is a story where some family just stopped speaking to their other family out of nowhere. For *ten* years they wouldn't acknowledge any of their attempts to reach out. Finally it came out that they had seen a photo book in the their home of a wedding and thought that they hadn't been invited. What really happened was they were the best man and maid of honor at their *friends'* wedding and since they had eloped earlier that year, their friends offered their photographer as a gift to them to take some wedding pictures. If their family had asked them, they would have shared their perfectly logical explanation, but they didn't ask. Satan definitely loves to divide us and isolate us and destroy relationships and he usually uses deception to do it. This lie could have easily been replaced with truth had they communicated their concern instead of letting these feelings turn into bitterness and anger.

That's exactly what happened to me. Dominic had been remodeling a condo down on Fifth Avenue so with the long commute and the long hours of finishing this project, we hadn't seen much of him. I started thinking about how much he works and how much overhead his shop/showroom costs and I got MAD. I was so cold and distant with him and when he had to work again the next morning I was ready to blow. The thing was, I *knew* I was being irrational. Less than a month before this when we all wrote thank you cards to our husbands, I actually thanked him for working so hard for us and being a man of his word to his clients. Now I'm going to resent him for it? I knew this was an attack because although I felt too angry to pinpoint the lie, the feelings I had were too intense… do you know what I mean? Have you ever been so upset and knew you really weren't justified in it? Or been so angry but didn't really even know why? On a Moody radio interview with Tim Muelhoff about his book "*Defending Your Marriage: The Reality of Spiritual Battle[1]*," Tim said there were five ways you can recognize you are under demonic attack:

Inappropriate anger

You start questioning God, His goodness or if He's for you

You start feeling lots of shame and having really negative feelings about yourself

You have violent dreams or lustful dreams that aren't with your spouse

You have feelings of impending doom, financial ruin, etc.

I ended up reaching out to a couple of friends and asked for prayer because this felt big and unreasonable and I needed some clarity, peace and truth. While I was waiting for their response, I got into the Word and wouldn't you know the exact chapter I was reading next ended with the verse that we have "the mind of Christ"(1 Cor. 2:16). I asked for Jesus' thoughts and as my friends responded to tell me they were praying, I prayed right along with them. I need you to hear me on this: sometimes you need to reach out to other believers when you're in this situation. Satan loves for us to feel alone. I've said that before because it's true. Satan can have fair game to influence our minds when we aren't bringing our thoughts to Christ, or asking another believer who will point us to the truth of God's Word to stand with us in battle. Again, this is why a group like this is important and this is why having people in your life who you can be accountable to (and also blatantly honest with about your sin, struggles or irrational thoughts) is absolutely imperative.

After a lot of prayer, reading scripture, asking for help from other believers, and choosing to worship God despite my thoughts by playing a worship playlist on my phone, something broke. I still felt the need to talk to Dominic but there was no anger in me. I felt like I needed to tell him the lies and that I was feeling anxious and afraid lately. He immediately prayed over me then asked what was worrying me. I told him I was worried we'd never get out of this overhead and with him working so much that we weren't connecting or on the same page. Can you believe God gave us an *hour* of time to ourselves that morning to hash everything out? That's a legit miracle in our house but both babies took a nap and our oldest was listening to an audio book. Dom reassured me he had a plan to streamline the business so we wouldn't need as big of a space but that he had to finish this project first. He also reassured me we had two weeks left of crazy and then we had a nice break between jobs over the holidays. One conversation completely revealed that the things I was anxious and angry about were completely *unnecessary* to be anxious or angry about. We went to church afterwards and as we sang worship songs together holding hands I honestly felt so thankful that even though the enemy might *form* a weapon against us, God's word says in Isaiah 54:17 that it won't prosper.

I'm not writing so much about spiritual warfare and Satan to scare you. We don't have to be scared of him because Jesus is stronger than him and where Satan's power is limited, Jesus' power is unlimited. And Jesus lives in *you* and Romans 8:37 says we are "more than conquerors through Him who loved us." However, we *do* need to be aware. We need to be alert (1 Peter 5:8). We need to read and follow what scripture says and arm ourselves each day for battle (Ephesians 6) because whether you believe it or not, we *are* in a war. We need to have accountability and people we can reach out to for prayer. We need to remember that not all our thoughts are our own but that Satan can plant thoughts in our heads. That's why it's so important to stay rooted in God's Word so we can replace lies with truth. We need to remember our spouse isn't our enemy because we do not fight against flesh and blood (Ephesians 6:12). And while we're on the subject, if you are feeling particularly angry towards your spouse, I want you to really stop and question whether or not Satan might be the instigator. Do you know what I realized over the past couple years? The times where I feel most upset at Dom (especially without something specific that happened), was usually an indicator that he might be having a stressful day. And sure enough, when we were talking that day, I realized just how much he had on his plate and I was *so* thankful I didn't lash out at him and add even more like I used to! It took me a while to figure this out! But Satan doesn't fight fair and comes at us even harder when we're tired, sick or stressed. If Dom is having a hard time, wouldn't it be just like the enemy to try and make him feel worse by using me against him? I don't want to be a vessel for Satan's scheming, but a vessel of love and peace for Jesus!

Lord, Your Word says in James 4:7 to "humble yourselves before God. Resist the devil and he will flee from you." He has no authority in our lives or marriages because You set us free with the blood of Christ. We pray that we would be quick to recognize Satan's schemes and quick to bring our thoughts captive to obey Jesus. We pray You would tear down strongholds in our minds and marriages, provide accountability in our lives so we aren't isolated, and give us a hunger for Your Word like never before so we can replace lies with truth and grow to know You more. We thank You for Jesus and that through Him we are more than conquerors. It's in His powerful name we pray, Amen.

EMAIL 38
WHO'S IN THE MIDDLE?

I was speaking with Spencer's mom, Pam, this week and she was telling me about an analogy I wanted to share with you.

Imagine a couple sitting together on a couch and a person squeezing in between the two of them. He starts whispering to the husband, "She just doesn't understand you. She doesn't get how hard you work. She doesn't respect you"

Then he turns his attention to the wife and starts saying, "He never helps you around the house. He just isn't romantic with you like he used to be. He doesn't love you well."

You can imagine the couple who was originally content on the couch with one another start to tense up as they listened to these words. The words weren't true or indicative of what one person thought of the other, but once those accusations were in their heads, the spouses begin to entertain them and their countenance towards one another reflects the change.

She said that the point of the illustration was to show how the enemy can get in the middle and try to pit you against your spouse and vice versa by trying to put thoughts in your head. The key is to recognize the thought and not entertain it any further. In fact scripture says, "We demolish arguments and every pretension that sets itself up against the knowledge of God, and we take captive every thought to make it obedient to Christ" (2 Corinthians 10:5).

I had a real life experience with this this week and realized how important it is. I literally got upset with Dom for leaving his dishes on the table and my mind immediately filled with all the ways I help around the house and he doesn't. Almost forgetting my little lesson from earlier, I went into the bathroom before I could act out on those thoughts and just prayed. I prayed Jesus would take over and take these thoughts captive and give me eyes to see my husband the way He wants me to see him. It wasn't an immediate fix but within an hour or so, all I could think of were the ways Dom loves on our boys, always treats me with kindness and gentleness and what a hard worker he is for our family. It made the dirty dish look completely ridiculous and I was so relieved I hadn't listened to those thoughts and picked a fight.

We have a very real enemy who would like nothing more than to cause strife in our relationships. When he distracts us by attacking our peace, this can take our focus off of what we should be doing. Just because you're thinking something doesn't mean that thought came from you, and it doesn't mean that the thought is true. If there is chaos and confusion going on, you can be certain that Satan is involved. And don't forget: he HATES marriage. He will come at you in any way he can to try and get you to turn on your spouse. Don't let him! The key to peace is focusing on Christ and thinking of things we can be grateful for. I leave you these verses out of Ephesians 4:2-3, and I pray them over each one of you: "Be completely humble and gentle; be patient, bearing with one another in love. Make every effort to keep the unity of the Spirit through the bond of peace."

We *can* take our thoughts captive and we *can* focus on the good in our spouse instead of the bad. It goes back to loving and not controlling. Letting God do the convicting and then focusing on the areas we need to work on in ourselves. Weed your own garden and quit trying to be Holy Spirit Junior.

Jesus tells us in John 14:27, "Peace I leave with you; my peace I give you. I do not give to you as the world gives. Do not let your hearts be troubled and do not be afraid."

Lord, would You allow the peace of Christ to rule in our marriages? Would You remind us that YOU are to be in the middle, above, beside and behind our marriages? We need You to infiltrate every part! We have an enemy that prowls around us like a lion but You are stronger than Him. As much as he wants us to fail, You want us to succeed that much more and we know that with You as the head of our marriage, we can do just that! We can forgive and love and encourage our spouses with Your grace. May we leave them and any change we think necessary up to You and focus more on what You want to do in us personally. May we focus more on how we can be a better spouse than on how they should be. May the cycle of selfishness end with us. We ask all of this in the powerful name of Christ Jesus our King, Amen.

EMAIL 39
WHAT KIND OF LOVER
ARE YOU?

Get your mind out of the gutter! Not that kind! Haha. I meant conditional or unconditional.

I like to think I'm unconditional (the agape kind of love God shows us…unwavering and not dependent on behavior) but truth be told, people are so much easier to love when they are behaving the way I want them to. Not sure if any of you watch "This is Us," but in one episode, one of the characters was accusing the mother of loving one of the siblings more than the other. She argued that she loved everyone equally but eventually broke down and cried, "It was just easier to love him! He didn't recoil when I touched him or abandon me when your father died!"

This was convicting not only as a wife but as a mother, daughter, sister, and friend. Early on in our marriage (and in my marriage with Spencer too!) if we got in a bad fight, I would start imagining how I could do life without them. I'd start adding up the money in our bank account, think about moving and in my mind say good riddance! I don't need this! I don't need YOU! To the point that Spencer even said one time "I know you're over there thinking you don't need me but you do and I need you too so just knock it off." It totally freaked me out! I thought he was a mind reader! This is really hard to admit to you because the dark parts of our thought life can be pretty hideous. But thankfully over time the Lord convicted me and exposed those lies as being contrary to His word. If I'm to love my husband with unconditional love like Christ loves me, then there should be no way out of this marriage, even mentally! I have to give it my all, lay down my life for him and prefer him to all others. That is our privilege and our calling and it is completely independent of our feelings or their behavior. Sometimes there are phases in your marriage where you feel "in love" and sometimes you have to choose to love. The Lord even goes so far as to take the guess work out of it by commanding us to love: "So now I am giving you a new commandment: Love each other. Just as I have loved you, you should love each other" (John 13:34).

Paul Tripp said in a DVD session at one of our meetings that it's "easy to be kind when our spouses are being a vehicle to what we want but it's harder when they become an obstacle."[1] So how do we stay consistent? Good news is that you don't have to white-knuckle it or fake it. In John 7:38 Jesus says, "Anyone who believes in me may come and drink! For the Scriptures declare, 'Rivers of living water will flow from his heart." I absolutely love this. I envision Jesus' love, peace, and strength flowing through me non-stop so that I become a conduit of all of His goodness to those around me. My only responsibility in this is to not "dam up" this river with sin and lies. When we root ourselves in Christ by spending time with Him, delighting in Him and asking Him to fill us with His love and Spirit, we can then have the overflow to love onto our spouse and the others in our lives and not give them our fickle human kind that ebbs and flows (or dams up!) with feelings and circumstances.

I liked what the patheos website had to say about unconditional love:

> Because we measure love by human standards, it can be hard to imagine what it means to be loved unconditionally. We understand passionate love, and young love, and first loves. Yet all three of those circle back towards the ability to sustain that love, and to most people there will come a time when that begins to feel difficult. The rush wears off, the facades come down, and daily life begins to wear down the sparkle. The ones who make it, are those who choose to hold on to that first kind of love, in all moments—even when the ones we are called to love seem entirely unlovable. To some small degree, that is the way God loves us. He holds on tightly to us, even when the going gets tough, and loves us at our very best and our lowest worst. His is a love with no earthly match, but an example of the way we should aspire to be. *Your*

love, O LORD, reaches to the heavens, your faithfulness to the skies. *Psalm 36:5-7* The best relationships are built on a foundation of love and trust. When we believe that we are secure and cherished, we feel stronger and more able to give that love out to the world. That is what God's faithful love should enable us to do on a grander scale. When we remain rooted in the security of His love, we are enabled to give it out freely to others.[2]

Father God, Your word says in 2 Timothy 1:7 that You give us a spirit of love, power and self-control. We thank you in particular for the spirit of love today and pray that we would extend the love You give to us to our husbands by the power of Your Spirit. We pray we would give our husbands the gift of safety, knowing we aren't going anywhere because that's the gift You give to us. We pray we would give them the gift of freedom so they may rest in the security that we are choosing to be in this marriage no matter what just like You chose us to be in covenant with You no matter what. We pray we would love and hold tight to this most important human relationship whether we feel like it or not. We pray we would be reminded by Your Spirit to call or text them today while we're apart to remind them of our unwavering love and of Yours. It's in the powerful name of Your son Jesus Christ that we ask these things. Amen.

EMAIL 40
TAKE YOUR MARRIAGE
TEMPERATURE

Have you taken your temperature lately? Not your exact body temperature but your marriage temperature. Last week I was struggling with being lukewarm. I hadn't seen much of Dom because February is our busiest month of the year for the business. One of my love languages is quality time so when I don't feel like we have had a chance to connect, I tend to think he must not care and then I decide I will try not to care right back at him. Because I'm really mature like that. I guess the bright side is that because of my *many* flaws, I have endless material for these e-mails! Ha.

Anyway, feeling guilty about my apathy, I climbed into bed Tuesday night and pulled out my *Sacred Marriage* book by Gary Thomas. I had never finished the last two chapters and boy did the Lord use that to both bless me and convict me!

> Use your dissatisfaction - or even your boredom with life and with your relationships- as a compass that directs you to the True North of your heart's passion: God himself. Remind yourself that in serial marriage the same process will inevitably repeat itself: great excitement, the thrill of discovery, and then, on some level increasing disillusionment. Let your relationship with your spouse point you to what you really need most of all: God's love and active presence in your life. Above all, don't blame your spouse for lack of fulfillment; blame yourself for not pursuing a fulfilling relationship with God....Marital dissatisfaction, on whatever level, is best met with the prayer, *'That's why I need you God.'* We are reminded of the transcendent ache in our soul that even this one very special person can't relieve entirely on their own. As odd as it may sound, I have discovered in my own life that my satisfaction or dissatisfaction with my marriage has

far more to do with my relationship to God than it does with my relationship to Lisa. **When my heart grows cold toward God, my other relationships suffer, so if I sense a burgeoning alienation from or lack of affection toward my wife, the first pace I look is how I'm doing with the Lord. Lisa is, quite literally, my God thermometer.**[1]

Boom. Dominic is my God-thermometer. If I'm feeling lukewarm or apathetic towards him, chances are I'm feeling that way towards Jesus too. My first thought was, *Nuh-uh! I'm just fine with you God! He's the one I'm not connecting with!* But the moment I truly examined my heart, I realized my time with the Lord had been severely lacking. I had replaced my quiet time with Him with cleaning, homeschooling, or napping (our youngest has decided to wake up every couple of hours lately!). Indeed, this area of my life that *supplies* life and love to all *other* areas of my life was not getting the attention it needs for me to have the mind and heart I *need.* I decided to put this to the test. The next morning I got up and had my time with Jesus and was in the Bible first thing before anything else could crowd out that time. I asked Him to help me put Him first in my thoughts and actions and wouldn't you know, I wasn't just seeing Dom differently, I was seeing my kids differently, my neighbors, and my friends. My apathy was replaced with affection, and the warmth and connection I had with my husband was especially refreshing and meaningful. We ended up talking and praying together more than we had in weeks and even falling asleep in each other's arms like we were newlyweds again. I felt like I'd truly discovered a secret and couldn't wait to share it with you.

Take your temperature. Use your spouse as your God-thermometer. Are you hot? Cold? Lukewarm? Pursue Jesus. He's been pursuing you whether you noticed or not. Receive and reciprocate that love and watch your marriage directly benefit. I'm not sure why I'm so shocked by this. The answer to truly everything is more of Jesus.

My prayer for each of you this week and for your spouses is really Paul's prayer:

For this reason I kneel before the Father, from whom every family in heaven and on earth derives its name. I pray that out of His glorious riches He may strengthen you with power through His Spirit in your inner being, so that Christ may dwell in your hearts through faith. And I pray that you, being rooted and established in love, may have power, together with all the Lord's holy people, to grasp how wide and long and high and deep is the love of Christ, and to know this love that surpasses knowledge—that you may be filled to the measure of all the fullness of God. (Ephesians 3:14–19).

EMAIL 41
YOUR HUSBAND DOESN'T
NEED TO LOVE YOU

One of our *WWC* meetings totally rocked me in the best possible way. I left there so incredibly refreshed and encouraged for a lot of reasons but one of them was an amazing video we heard from Paul Tripp. He said something profound:

> You don't *need* your husband to love you to be a good wife. And husbands, you don't *need* your wife to respect you to be a good husband. You have everything you need in Christ to be the loving and kind spouse the Lord wants you to be. You can pray that your husband will love you. You can pray for your wife to respect you. But those are not pre-requisites or needs in order for you to be a good spouse.[1]

You. Have. Everything. You. Need. IN JESUS! It's His power, His might and His love that will enable you to be a good spouse. 2 Peter 1:3 says, "By His divine power, God has given us everything we need for living a godly life. We have received all of this by coming to know Him, the one who called us to Himself by means of his marvelous glory and excellence."

So often we feel entitled. We feel self-pity. And those lead to a downward spiral of thinking we "need" more than we are given. But marriage is not about *us*! It's about the covenant we made with God and how we treat and honor that covenant represents Him to our spouse, our children, our family, our friends and our neighbors. And our time on this earth is not about our comfort but about His kingdom so don't worry if life isn't going the way you thought it would. We have an eternity of comfort if we have received Jesus as Lord of our lives. The only thing we can't do in Heaven that we can do here is proclaim the gospel. And one of the best places to do that is within our own marriages. While we are here, we are to pour ourselves out in service to Him and to others. If Christ, the God of heaven and earth did not come to be served but to serve and give his life as a ransom for many (Mathew 20:28), then how can we possibly make this life of ours or this marriage (or anything really!) about us? "For you were bought with a price. So glorify God in your body" (1 Corinthians 6:20). Our behavior, our love, our service is not dependent on anyone else's behavior because Christ gives us all we need to live a godly life. What freedom!!!!

C.S. Lewis said, "If God is Love, He, by definition, is something more than mere kindness. And it appears from all records, that though He has often rebuked us and condemned us, He has never regarded us with contempt. He has paid us the intolerable compliment of loving in the deepest, most tragic, most inexorable sense."[2] He loves you deeply so you can love others deeply.

Heavenly Father, thank You for these incredible women who are doing the hard work of making their marriage a priority. I pray that You would bless them. Lord, I pray that we would love and respect our husbands with Your inexorable love and that they would love and respect us in return. But I thank You that regardless of our circumstances, we have all we need in You to live a godly life and that we are not dependent on anyone or anything other than You, the One who never changes and is the same yesterday today and forever. We praise You and love You and thank You that You are in control, that You are for us and not against us and that we are the apple of your eye. It's in Jesus' powerful name that we ask these things. Amen.

EMAIL 42
FEELING OVERWHELMED?

When feeling overwhelmed, it's usually a good indicator that our priorities have gotten out of whack. Let's review what our list of priorities are:

First: GOD!!! He really gets His own list but He should always be number one! If our relationship or time with Him is neglected, a downward spiral will eventually occur. Apart from Him we can do nothing (John 15:5) and when we are disconnected from Him, essentially we are starving ourselves. He is bread for our souls and the living water we need to have a healthy spiritual life. Disconnection is usually accompanied by increased feelings of anxiety, hopelessness, irritability and then sin quickly sneaks in--increasing those feelings even more! When we make our time with Him a priority, we see things with a proper perspective and every part of our life benefits from the love, peace, joy and guidance we receive from Him.

Second: HUSBAND! It's so easy to let kids and jobs and ministry and hobbies creep their way up our list and replace the guy that has become so familiar to us. We often justify it consciously or subconsciously thinking, "Well, he will always be here" or "I will make it up to him later" or "I'm too tired and I don't feel like I'm his priority so why should I make him mine?" This is where the enemy can come in like crazy. When we let our guard down, Satan puts his foot in. We have to work at keeping our spouse in their rightful place, preferring him to all others. This isn't easy! But it pays off in dividends with a healthy marriage and an example for your children to look up to and emulate.

Third: We don't usually have trouble with the third. The third usually tries to usurp one or two. So insert your third here. Kids, work, ministry, etc. and then go on down the list from there. The main thing is keeping God number one and spouse number two. When those are in order, the rest often work themselves out on their own.

I've been feeling overwhelmed the past two weeks and if I'm honest, my priorities haven't been in order. Revisiting that list is important and convicting. I'm working on prioritizing God, my husband and my kids one hour and one day at a time and if there's time or room for anything else, then by the power of Christ within me I can address those.

Lord, please give us the grace to put You first. When we focus on the command of loving You with all of our hearts and loving our neighbor as ourselves all the other commandments take care of themselves. When we focus on the proper order of our priority list it is much the same. We pray You would convict us if anything has usurped the proper order You have set up for us and we ask Your forgiveness for that. With Your strength we walk forward asking You to help us love You and our spouse and our children with agape love. We give You our chaos and confusion, our anxiety and our feelings of being overwhelmed and we ask You to please replace it with peace and clarity. Amen.

EMAIL 43
BE HIS SOFT PLACE

Today as I was putting on a long sleeve sweater and some warm fuzzy socks, I was comforted by the softness of each item. It was inviting against the harsh cold.

In my quiet time a bit later on, the Lord put it on my heart to pray for softness towards Dominic this week. I felt plenty soft towards him so I wasn't sure why, but I got to thinking that I usually feel all "warm and fuzzy" about him on Mondays. We've had time to connect over the weekend and talk so I understand where his heart is and what he is struggling with. I usually *start* out pretty soft but as the trials and hardships pile up over the week, I tend to feel a disconnect with him and become more self-focused with my own struggles. Or I become irritated with him because I'm feeling overwhelmed, totally forgetting he is dealing with his own struggles and things that overwhelm him as well.

An example of this is our house hunt. We have seen dozens of homes over the last few weeks and it is emotionally and physically draining on top of all our normal responsibilities. With every prospective home we are wondering, "Can we live here? Would this be a good spot for the kids? Does this feel like home?" I literally want to eat anything chocolate and take a nap after each outing and we are both really tired. A couple of the houses we've seen had the potential to join our home and our business in one location. The last one we really thought was "it," until we actually visited it and realized the photographer of the home was a genius. Or a criminal. Ha! Needless to say the pictures were misleading. Dominic who is quite literally *always* happy and rarely fazed by much let out a huge sigh on the way home. He shared that not only has he been trying to picture moving our home, but also potentially moving his business which is even more mentally draining to figure out all the details. I hadn't even *thought* about how that added an extra thick layer of stress to this already stressful situation but I was immediately softened towards him.

I wanted to give him a huge hug and tell him everything would work out, but we were driving so I just held his hand and reassured him as best I could (which is a real role reversal considering I've been straight up nuts in this whole process! Pregnancy + house hunting = tearful lunatic in maternity pants).

Every time our husbands step out the front door, they enter a harsh, cold world with much different expectations put on them than we face. They are constantly asked, "What do you do?" and the pressure they feel to provide is *strong* because that is how our culture defines them on a daily basis. This pressure is much more intense than I think we are capable of understanding because our role as women is not solely defined by work like theirs tends to be. If they face harshness, judgments, pressure and conflict all day, the last thing they want to feel when they come home is any of those aforementioned things. I realized when he shared his struggle in this whole process with me that that is just the tip of the iceberg. There is so much more he probably internalizes and protects me from. As women, we tend to communicate our difficulties more because there is less judgment and by nature, we resolve things by talking them out. We have friends, sisters and mothers we can be transparent with. We aren't expected to keep a stiff upper lip like they are. When men get together, they tend to discuss surface subjects like sports or work or cars. It's hard to get in their heads and even harder if *we* are "hard."

I loved how the Lord used tangible, comforting things this morning to remind me to be that soft place for Dom and even more to pray that He would help me be that for him. Tonight I want to try and make our home warm, like a sanctuary for him. Can you imagine how quickly you would want to come home if you knew you were loved and accepted no matter what? The prayer I taped on my wall today is the same prayer I have for all of us:

Father God, thank You that You are so intimate and so real. You speak to us just like any good father wants to speak to his children. If we feel sometimes as though You are silent, I pray that You would show us anything that is keeping us or hindering us from hearing You. It's often not that You aren't speaking, but that we aren't listening. Thank You for the reminder today to take time to be still with You, like a little girl sitting on her daddy's lap while he tells her a story. Thank You for telling me to be soft. To be warm, welcoming and loving to my husband. I pray for each woman reading this that you would give her eyes to see her spouse the way You see him. That you would give us supernatural insight into their struggles, spoken or silent. That you would give us a compassion, empathy and softness towards them so we can be a safe place for them. Lord, I ask that You would unite us, connect us and remind us we are a team this week and if we are being harsh with them, we are really being harsh with ourselves because we are one. Fill us with Your Spirit so that we may be strengthened and encouraged and so that we may love our husbands completely and unconditionally by Your grace and power. Remind us of our identity in You. In my time with You today, You reminded me I'm your daughter and a temple of the Living God, so I pray right now by the power of Your Word that You would remind these precious sisters of mine of that truth as well, so that we can love and live in light of who we truly are. "For we are the temple of the living God. As God said:'I will live in them and walk among them. I will be their God, and they will be my people. Therefore, come out from among unbelievers, and separate yourselves from them, says the LORD. Don't touch their filthy things, and I will welcome you. And I will be your Father, and you will be my sons and daughters, says the LORD Almighty'" (2 Corinthians 6:16-18). It's in the name of our Advocate and Savior Jesus Christ that we ask these things, Amen.

EMAIL 44
THE DANGER OF IN-LAWS

When I was a little girl, my grandmother was heavily involved in our lives. For the most part, it seemed wonderful but what I didn't realize until later was that she often pointed out my dad's flaws to my mom and at the pinnacle of their marriage crisis, she encouraged my mom to move from Florida to Tennessee with all four of us children and start a new life. She even paid for the house and business my mom would have there. They divorced and although my dad eventually followed us there and they re-married, it wasn't until they distanced themselves from her influence that their marriage began to thrive. I'm not blaming my grandmother. She grew up in a home with an abusive stepdad and married an abusive husband. She didn't trust men because the only ones she'd ever had in her life had hurt her. But her distrust became my mom's distrust and to this day, I often have to replace lies and tear down strongholds that were unknowingly passed down to me. "We use God's mighty weapons, not worldly weapons, to knock down the strongholds of human reasoning and to destroy false arguments" (2 Corinthians 10:4). When someone is consistently criticizing your spouse, you find yourself either constantly defending them (which is exhausting) or you find their doubts creeping in and becoming your own.

There are two other families I know where the parents of each child came in between the couple and now each of those adult children are divorced and living with their parents while the children are shuffled back and forth. There is a reason scripture warns us of this and tells us in Matthew 19:4 to "leave and cleave." The husband/wife relationship is stronger then the parent/child ("Therefore a man shall leave his father and his mother and hold fast to his wife, and they shall become one flesh." Genesis 2:24).

One of the most detrimental things we can do is to share our marriage struggles with our parents or run home when things get tough. We are putting them, ourselves and our spouses in a terrible situation. They can't be objective because they will only be able to feel *protective* of their child. And when the problem is solved or you have made up, they might not even know that took place so while things are better for you, they are still left with all of that worry and anger. It's not fair to them and it's not fair to your spouse. When you plant a seed of negativity or complain about your spouse to them, you are poisoning them against your spouse whether you mean to or not. In addition, the devil can bring that seed back up *through* them long after the fight is over causing a cycle of un-forgiveness and resentment when they remind you of previous fights and issues.

When you have a problem, you take it to God, your spouse, a pastor, a trusted friend whose life is founded on the word of God, or a sound biblical counselor if further help is needed. They *can* be objective where your family cannot. You have to remember that it is Jesus, you, your spouse (and your children if you have them) who are a unit and that's the unit you must prioritize and protect at all costs.

You need people who will advocate for your marriage, not argue against it. If you find yourself in the extremely difficult situation of having in-laws who are damaging your relationship, think *triage*. You need to get yourself into an emergency room and the only people allowed in are the doctor (Jesus) and the patients (you and your spouse) because this situation requires immediate attention. If your parents or his parents cannot respect your spouse or your marriage, there needs to be some strong and clear boundaries set of what you expect from them. You can set these in love but they must be adhered to. It is not up to you whether they adhere to them or not but it is up to you to defend those boundaries and perhaps distance yourself from them until they follow suit. I know that sounds drastic but this is your marriage, your covenant with God, and you should be drastic when it comes to protecting it. You want to show grace just like we are shown, but don't let the word "grace" be an excuse for you or your spouse to be abused by them.

Father God, we made a covenant with You and our spouse to love one another through better or worse. I pray that in the worse we wouldn't take those problems unfairly to our family but we would take them to You and ask for Your help. I pray You would help us to leave our families and cleave to our spouses the way Your word says. I thank You for Your word that warns us, convicts us and guides us with the principles that will lead to healthy relationships. May we not just read them but apply them in our lives by Your grace. Thank You for our families. We pray we would love them with Your love but also have the proper boundaries necessary to protect this most important covenant that represents Your love towards us. We ask this in the name of Jesus, Amen.

EMAIL 45
NO MARRIAGE IS HOPELESS

Tony Evans said this recently in a sermon about marriage: "Is your marriage dead? No problem. We serve a God who was raised from the dead. Death is nothing for Him. And neither is a dead marriage. He can resurrect your marriage. Any marriage. And give it NEW life. Give you a better marriage than you ever had before."[1]

That's the amazing news about Jesus. Death has no hold. And guess what?! "The Spirit of God, who **raised** Jesus from the dead, lives in you. And just as God **raised** Christ Jesus from the dead, He will give life to your mortal bodies by this **same** Spirit living within you" (Romans 8:11e [emphasis mine]).

There is no problem too big. No marriage too far gone. It can be dead and buried. Divorce papers signed and He can *still* give it new life. That fact should give us such confidence and peace for the future! I know that *everyone* can go through difficult times but we don't have to fear if we are in that place, or be afraid of ever getting to that place, because if you are in Christ, nothing is too difficult for Him.

I've shared with you before about Spencer's parents, the Greenlees. In their marriage ministry, they have seen everything you can think of from abuse to adultery. Did you know the people who started the ministry they serve in (Married for Life) were actually divorced? He'd had an affair. Moved out. But she still stayed single and prayed for their marriage for *three years*. Eventually he gave his life to Christ, they remarried and have been sharing their story with others and started a marriage ministry that is now international and has served millions. If you ask them, no marriage is hopeless! They have just seen God show up too many times to have any doubt about that.

You might be thinking "It's not me! I'm willing to work on it! He's given up!" If that's the case, I'd encourage you to remember

Saul in the book of Acts and how Jesus took him from being the worst persecutor of the Christian people to the best missionary of all time who wrote the majority of the New TestAment. It took Jesus' voice and three days of blindness to change this man. Jesus can redeem anyone and He knows exactly what it will take to bring us to Himself.

You are a new creation in Christ and your marriage can be a new creation as well. Hold onto that hope because it's a secure one. Don't lose hope because we serve the God *of* Hope.

Now, in the words of Paul himself in Romans 15:13:

"I pray that God, the source of hope, will fill you completely with joy and peace because you trust in him. Then you will overflow with confident hope through the power of the Holy Spirit."

EMAIL 46
TWO WORLDS

There is an amazing book my friend Kate turned me onto about a year ago called *Prayer: Does It Make Any Difference?* by Phillip Yancey. He addresses so many hard questions and his writing style is very straight-forward, intelligent but most of all, honest. In one of my favorite parts of this book he talks about two different worlds:

> When I pray, it may seem that I am narrowing my world, retreating from the real world into a prayer closet in Jesus' metaphor. Actually I am entering into another world, just as real but invisible, a world that has power to change both me and the world I seem to be retreating from. Regular prayer helps me to protect inner space, to prevent the outer world from taking over....Contact with God doesn't just provide a moment of spiritual ecstasy; it equips me for the rest of life. I corral a few minutes of calm in the morning in hopes that I can carry some part of that calm into the rest of the day. If I pray consistently I feel free and strong, able to meet the challenges and temptations of the day. As the book of Psalms demonstrates so well, prayer does not mean retreating away from life, but rather bringing the stuff of our world—the rhythms of nature, harassing problems, disturbed emotions, personality conflicts — before God, then asking for a new perspective and new energy to take back to that world....In short, prayer invites God into my world and ushers me into God's. Jesus himself, who spent many hours in solitary prayer, invariably returned to a busy world of weddings, dinners, and crowds of sick and needy people.[1]

I often feel as though I just want to escape, and time with the Lord certainly provides for that! But what I love even more is that when I have to "go back," He is going with me and this time He is giving me His eyes to see the problems and trials. It's often like wearing a dirty pair of sunglasses. Everything looks smudged and scratched and confusing but time with Him clears away the yuck and allows us to see clearly. When we face things in light of His power and love and remember that the God of the Universe who has endless resources *also* has endless love for us, it makes the world seem a little less chaotic knowing He goes before us and behind us ("You go before me and follow me. You place your hand of blessing on my head." Psalm 139:5).

Father, we come to You now to take a break from this world. We lift up our husbands to You and the other pressing things in our lives and as we come back, I pray we would remember You are with us. Lord, Your word says You are able to do immeasurable more than we can ask or imagine (Ephesians 3:20-21) and this life and this world are all Yours. Everything is truly about You, not us...what a relief! It takes all the pressure off. Lord, how can we join You in what You are up to? How can we work with You in our marriages, our parenting, our jobs, our neighborhood and our churches? If we are still breathing it is because You are still doing a work in us and still have work for us to do. We come to You and rely on You for direction, peace, strength and love. In Jesus' name we pray, Amen.

EMAIL 47
UNCONDITIONAL RESPECT

We had a recent meeting that was so awesome I wanted to go over some of what went down for two reasons: if you were there, you probably want some of those highlights reiterated (like me! There were so many good things I want them *etched* in my brain forever!) and if you weren't there, every wife should hear this at some point in their lives.

We watched session five of our *Love and Respect*[1] series and Dr. Emmerson Eggerichs (the author of the amazing and marriage-changing book, *Love and Respect*[2]) interviewed a woman who for *eight* years felt like her marriage was hopeless. She said she was ready to leave, even asked a friend to help her plan an escape to a hotel for her and the kids, but that friend showed up and said she didn't want to help her get out of her marriage but to stay in it and fight for it. She was mad at the friend at the time but said she needed someone to speak truth in her life at that moment.

The woman from the interview had started reading the book *Love and Respect* and basically thought, "What do I have to lose?" She started applying the biblical principal of unconditional respect found in 1 Peter 3:1-2: "Likewise, wives, be subject to your own husbands, so that even if some do not obey the word, they may be won without a word by the conduct of their wives, when they see your respectful and pure conduct."

She said she didn't want to do this. She didn't feel like showing her husband respect. He didn't deserve it! But the Word of God didn't say to do it if he deserved it or not. In fact, it says even if he is disobedient, he can be won over by your respectful conduct. She was frustrated but she knew what she was doing wasn't working and trusted God enough to give this a try. She started showing her husband respect regardless of his behavior.

In one example, they were in a fight and when he intentionally said something to push her buttons, she chose not to rise but respond with something kind. Dr. Eggerichs calls this, "Stopping the crazy cycle." She shows disrespect, he acts unloving. Or he acts unloving therefore she shows disrespect. When you are in a perpetual cycle of fighting and hurting each other, someone has to be the mature one and choose to stop, even if it means laying down your "rights." When someone chooses to respond with grace, humility, love, and respect instead of anger, bitterness and unkind words, then the cycle can actually stop. But someone has to choose to get off the crazy train and start implementing scripture despite how they may feel. Another thing she did was start to recognize the lies of the enemy faster. She always had a playlist on repeat of negative things about her husband and marriage. She said she had to "Recognize, Replace and Repeat." Recognize the negative thought or lie from Satan, replace it with the truth of God's word, and repeat it as often as necessary until that thought stopped. Two examples were " There is no hope for this marriage! It's impossible to save!" The truth she replaced it with is from Matthew 19:26 where Jesus tells us, "All things are possible with God." The other lie was, "I can't do this! It's just too hard!" The truth she replaced it with was from Philippians 4:13: "I can do all things through Christ who gives me strength." Before long, the truth would come to her mind instead of the lie or bad thought. This didn't happen overnight but now she and her husband are madly in love. "The Word of God works! You just have to apply it!" she said.

After the video, Kate set up a lovely fire pit outside where we were able to discuss what stood out to us before we ended with prayer. One wife brought up how we expect our husbands to love us unconditionally but when it comes to respecting them, we expect them to earn it which is not at all what this verse says. Another wife said how her husband told her she "says the nice words" but he can tell she doesn't really respect him based on her actions. What's a girl to do? What if your husband isn't doing something that you think is very respectable? Or what if you are on the crazy cycle and are so hurt and feel that you are right and he is wrong that you can't possibly be the one to lay down your pride and be nice when he's being awful?

It's only possible with the power of God. Our role in this is to surrender to the Lord and the truth of His Word. Sometimes the prayer goes something like, "Lord, I don't even *want* to pray about this! I don't even want You to help I'm so mad! But soften my heart, Lord. Help me *want* to want You to help. Help me *want* to want to pray. Help me respect him out of obedience to You Lord Jesus because obedience always precedes blessing. I trust that if You're asking me to do this it is for my good and for my peace." I was reading in 1 Corinthians 7 the other day and verse 23 (NLT) says, "God paid a high price for you, so don't be enslaved by the world." In Philippians 2:3-9 it says, "Do nothing from selfish ambition or conceit, but in humility count others more significant than yourselves. Let each of you look not only to his own interests, but also to the interests of others. Have this mind among yourselves, which is yours in Christ Jesus, who, though He was in the form of God, did not count equality with God a thing to be grasped, but emptied Himself, by taking the form of a servant, being born in the likeness of men. And being found in human form, He humbled himself by becoming obedient to the point of death, even death on a cross."

The King of all Kings gave up all His rights to come to earth and live the perfect life for us and die the death *we* deserved so we could spend eternity with Him. Jesus is the absolute, LITERAL embodiment of humility. And humility is going to be what it takes for you to have a successful marriage. This life isn't about us. This marriage isn't about us. It's all about Jesus. Our lives are His! We were bought at a price! There is such freedom in knowing that when we die to ourselves and give Him free reign to live through us, there is nothing we can't accomplish (even respecting our spouses unconditionally!). Do this as unto Him because it's what He asked you to do. Dr. Eggerich's says to imagine Jesus standing behind your husband and show him respect as if it's Jesus Himself you are respecting. When He calls us to something, we can always trust that at the very root of it, it is for our good, our peace and our joy. Even worship is like that! He wants us to worship Him because when we do, it puts all our problems in perspective because it reminds us of what a loving, powerful and capable God we serve. It replaces lies in our minds with truth. He has a purpose in everything and He is working all of those things for *your* good because *He* is good and He loves you more than you'll ever be able to grasp.

Lord, we pray that with this knowledge of what Your Word says about respect that we wouldn't just hear it, but that we would receive it and become doers of it by the power of Your Holy Spirit. We ask that You would remind us today of how much You love us so that we can overflow Your love onto our spouses. We ask that You would change our marriages for the better and that our words and actions would help our husbands feel respected. We love you, Jesus, and thank you for the example of humility You set for us. May we imitate You. In Your powerful name we pray.

EMAIL 48
PERSONALITY DIFFERENCES

In Psalm 139:14 David says "I praise You because I am fearfully and wonderfully made." Amen David! God made no mistakes when He knit us together in our mother's womb (Psalm 139:13) We all have different personality types and it's important in our marriages to understand not only how the Lord uniquely made us, but what kind of personality we each have so that we can understand each other better. By understanding where someone is coming from, or why they think a certain way, it allows for better communication, less frustration and more grace for us to show to one another. I heard a sermon once about the importance of studying your spouse. We should seek to "study them" and understand how the Lord made them which in turn will help us appreciate them more. Something that would be fun and beneficial for you to do together would be to take a couple of these personality tests. There are several, but I would recommend enneagram (https://www.enneagraminstitute.com/type-descriptions/) and DISC (https://www.123test.com/disc-personality-test/).

A third resource is a class called "GPS". It is a course you and your hubby can take together to discover how God made you and for what purpose. Dom and I did it over the summer and I gained such an in-depth understanding of his personality, strengths, spiritual gifting and goals afterwards (and vice versa!). It changed how we did life and business together. You can find out more here: http://www.gpslifejourney.com.

When you don't understand how your spouse is wired, it's like speaking to someone in Chinese when they speak French. There are a lot of unnecessary misunderstandings. We think they are looking at the situation the same way we are, or that they need love or encouragement the same way we do, because that is all we know. When you make a genuine effort to try and understand one another and how you both think and see things, you can begin to appreciate those differences, be strong for each other where the other is weak, and give grace to the areas where they struggle.

This can apply to our children and other important relationships as well. The best thing this did for me was make me feel OK for being me. For so many years I wished I were more decisive, less passionate/emotional in certain ways, less anxious, etc. I so badly wanted to be this laid back, zen, flowers in her hair, go with the breeze kind of gal who always made beautiful meals and scrapbooks and was organized. The real me tends to worry, burns most meals (or myself! Seriously. I have multiple scars) and has not made a single scrapbook in her life, including a baby book for Trooper who is 8 years old for crying out loud. But this is not how God wired me and not only is that OK, it's great! He wired me to want to go into foreign places to do missions, to write, do public speaking, to love the outdoors and lots of adventure. He made me and when I criticize myself, I criticize His handiwork. And when I criticize my hubby I am doing the same thing. Being intentional about understanding how God wired us gives us the freedom to look for the best in ourselves and our spouses and leave the parts that need changing in the Hands of the One who can actually do the changing.

Lord, thank You for making us each uniquely. There are not two fingerprints alike— that is how intentional You were to show us that each one of us is special to You. I pray You would show us the right tools to learn more about how You made us and how You made our spouse. I pray You would help us be less critical and that we would see each other through Your eyes. Thank you that as we learn more about them, we will start to appreciate them more and I pray You would reduce the frustration and miscommunication in our marriages as a result. You are so good, so worthy to praised and so faithful to meet us where we are and most of all love us where we are. Would You give us the grace to love You, seek You, know You and understand You more than ever before. In the name of Jesus I pray, Amen.

EMAIL 49
IS IT EVER OK TO FLIRT?

Is flirting with, or entertaining the thought of another man, ever ok? I think most of our gut reactions would be a resounding "no!" But are there areas in your life that need stronger boundaries? For example: what would you do if that ex-boyfriend emails you or Facebook messages you? What would you do if the guy at work gives you lots of compliments that anyone would want to hear? Should you allow a male massage therapist when getting a massage? What would you do if the man from your small group asks you to coffee to "talk about the Bible and pray?"

To keep our marriages safe, we need strict boundaries: physically *and* mentally. A rule of thumb is that there should be no spending time alone with the opposite sex unless it's your dad, brother, son or husband. Sounds drastic but drastic is what we need to protect our marriages! *Especially* in this present culture where there are infinite ways to communicate with the opposite sex. It can seem harmless, but can become harmful more quickly than you ever imagined.

There should also be no returning of messages or emails or taking calls from exes. Those relationships are in the past! A good question to ask is: would I want my husband to do this? Would I encourage my best friend to do this? Satan is looking for not only a foothold in our marriages but even a toehold! He just needs you to start thinking of that guy at work a bit more. Or entertaining the idea of "ministering" to a man that is not your spouse because in the mind is where adultery starts. It might seem innocent but how slippery that slope can be! The enemy seeks to *kill, steal,* or *destroy* (John 10:10). Do not give him any room to work with WHATSOEVER. Better be safe then sorry. Ask the question, "Can I ask Jesus to bless this action? This thought?" If not, ask Him to give you the strength to run from temptation! One of my favorite verses when I gave my life over to Jesus was 1 Corinthians 10:13: *"No temptation has overtaken you that is not common to man. God is faithful, and He will not let you be tempted beyond your ability,* but with the temptation He will also provide the way of escape, that you may be able to endure it." The temptations in your life are no different from what others experience. And God is faithful. He will not allow the temptation to be more than you can stand. When you are tempted, He will show you a way out so that you can endure. This has happened to me so many times. One such situation was as a very new Christian, I got an invitation to go out drinking with some friends. When I hung out with them, it never ended well. Our only reason for hanging out was to get drunk. I also found out an ex of mine was going to be out. I really wanted to see him. My life looked so different then it used to even a couple months prior but the temptation was strong and I literally felt like I was in a tug-o-war between my flesh and my spirit. I went ahead and got dressed but when I got in the car, a worship song was playing that reminded me that I was a new creation in Christ. I prayed with all my heart for the Lord to give me strength not to go, and with a strength that was not my own, I turned off my car and walked back into my house. Peace literally flooded my soul.

You might not be tempted in this exact moment, but if that day ever comes, knowing your boundaries will give you a great head start in addition to knowing scripture, which is how we fight lies and temptation...it's our sword! God will always provide a way out for you and whether your spouse knows or even appreciates the length you've gone to guard your precious covenant, the Lord knows and is cheering you on, giving you strength and fighting for you.

Lord Jesus, thank You that You equip us to fight temptation and sin. Thank You that You encourage us in Your word to guard our covenant with You and with our spouse. Thank You that You will always provide a way out no matter what Satan tries to throw at us and that stronger is He that is in us than he that is in the world (1 John 4:4). You have already overcome Satan and Your victory is our victory because You dwell inside us. You are our Savior, Defender, and Shield! In You we have everything, all fullness of joy, peace and most importantly, our salvation. We praise You, Lord. We lift up our spouses to You and ask that You would help us honor and respect them with our actions and words. We pray You would help us be the wives You want us to be and help them be the husbands You want them to be. Show us how to specifically love and encourage them this week and remind them they are the object of our affection on this earth, no other man. May we focus on You and be filled with Your love and spirit so we can be a blessing to them. In your powerful name, Jesus, Amen.

EMAIL 50
LIKE A SHEPHERD

A couple months ago I heard about a book on Moody Radio for husbands called *Like a Shepherd* by Robert Wolgemuth about leading their families like a shepherd. I heard very little of the interview but thought at the time it sounded like a great premise for a book and was reminded of this morning when I was reading through John 10 about Jesus being a good shepherd.

There are several places in scripture where we are referred to as sheep and that highlight what a good shepherd does: he lays down his life for his sheep, he goes after them if they are lost or being attacked, he feeds them and guides them and protects them, etc (Isaiah 40:11, John 10:11, Psalm 23).

As I was thinking about the author calling husbands to become good shepherds of their families, I thought of what a difficult and scary calling that would be. That's a lot of pressure to be responsible for the protection and provision of their wives and children! A pressure I think we forget they can carry. But the beauty of this whole thing is that they don't have to have that pressure if they look to the Good Shepherd as their example and learn to depend on Him to lead them.

All of this to say, I felt very led to pray for our husbands as the shepherds of our families this week. I want to pray for them that they would humbly submit to Christ leading them, that they would be quick to hear His voice and follow Him and that as they keep their eyes on Him. That through His example they learn what it truly means to be a good shepherd to the flock the Lord has entrusted to them.

Wherever your husband is in his walk right now with Christ, from non-existent to thriving, we can all pray for the Lord to meet him where he is, encourage him, comfort him and speak to him. We can pray that he would not try to take upon himself the heavy yoke of feeling the need to protect and provide for his family all on his own but to come to Christ, take on His yoke, and allow Jesus to do the heavy lifting. We can ask Jesus to show him what to do and how to do it and to walk through this life hand in hand with the Shepherd who is leading and guiding all who are His own.

Lord Jesus, our Good Shepherd, thank You that nothing or no one can snatch Your sheep out of Your hand (John 10:29). Thank You that whether our husbands are leading and guiding our families or not at this moment that You will always lead and guide us and protect us and there is never a moment where we can't turn to You or depend on You. Whenever we walk through the valley of the shadow of death, we need not fear because Your rod and staff will comfort us (Psalm 23) as You will never leave us or forsake us (Hebrews 13:5). Lord, we lift up our precious husbands to You right now. They are indeed precious in Your sight because You love them and know them. Will you encourage them to rest in You today? To press into You instead of giving into the pressure that surrounds them even at this very moment? Please, Jesus, remind them they need only depend on You for wisdom and guidance. Please drown out the other voices of the world, the enemy and even their own flesh and make Your voice the one they hear and respond to. Help them to supernaturally lead us in a way that brings You glory. Help us to not be rebellious or controlling sheep, but to submit to them as we submit to You because we can trust You to lead our husbands and our families. You willingly sacrificed Your own life for us, how can we ever doubt how much You love Your sheep? You are truly the Good Shepherd and we petition before You this day to lead and bless our husbands as they lead and bless our families by Your strength and not their own. Show us how we can specifically and intentionally be an encouragement to them this week. Please give us eyes to see them the way You do and give them eyes to see us that way too. It's in Your powerful and holy name we humbly ask these things, Amen.

EMAIL 51
WARRIOR WIVES CHALLENGE

I was thinking about the *Warrior Wives Club* today and a little wave of guilt came over me. Honestly, my prayer life last week gets a thumb down.

Did I even pray for my husband? Maybe I said something generic like, "Lord, please watch over him and bless his day," but not in a specific or contemplative way.

Was I encouraging to him? Not really. In fact I was relatively selfish, which I'm sure is a symptom of lack of prayer over his life and mine.

If I had been praying for him and aligning my heart with God's ("Draw near to God and He will draw near to you." James 4:8), I know I wouldn't have been as self-absorbed.

This week let's make a change! Let's be different! More specific, more intentional, more selfless. I'm challenging myself — and you! — to ask your husband what he would like you to be praying for during the week. Listen to him carefully (maybe even take notes!) and bring these things before the Lord every day this week. This week, there were several mornings where I was able to catch him before he left and pray. This quickly became a family event! Our little 2-year-old would come running from wherever he was, naked (because that's how he always is), and excited because he knows this is time for a group hug. Imagine a naked little bottom running as fast as he can go yelling, "Pray! Pray! Pray!" It literally makes us laugh out loud.

I would like us to compare our attitudes (and his attitude!) next week to the attitudes we displayed this past week. I suspect with fervent prayer they will be quite different. "This is the confidence we have in approaching God: that if we ask anything according to his will, he hears us." 1 John 5:14

Heavenly Father, I pray over each marriage represented here. You are holy, mighty, powerful and loving. And You are the biggest advocate for our marriages which so beautifully represent the covenant You made with us. The covenant that says You aren't going anywhere. Would you give us the grace to remind our spouses that we aren't going anywhere either? Would you remind us by the power of Your Spirit to pray for them in a way that is specific and loving and to prompt us to ask them how we can pray for them? Would you help us grow closer to You and closer to each other? We thank You for giving us these men and for the privilege of being married. We ask Your forgiveness for the times we've forgotten what a true privilege it really is. Please protect each woman reading this from any lies Satan is speaking to her about her marriage and replace it with truth. I ask this in the powerful name of Your son Jesus Christ. Amen.

EMAIL 52
DON'T STOP

I had a couple ideas for writing yesterday but nothing stuck. I decided not to send the email until I really felt led to share something He was putting on my heart. It didn't happen until around 11 pm last night and since then I have had this overwhelming feeling to encourage you that prayer changes things. A good friend (and fellow warrior wife!) told me recently that she's been believing the lie that her prayers are ineffective. As a result, she's seen a lot of unnecessary pain and chaos in her life and marriage. Let me tell you something: Your. Prayers. MATTER. They make a huge difference in your life and the lives of others and just like a parent wants his/her child to communicate with them, so does your Heavenly Father. He loves you and *wants* to hear from you and wants to help you. I read the most beautiful verse this morning in Psalm 37:23-24 (NLT): "The Lord directs the steps of the godly. He delights in every detail of their lives. Though they stumble, they will never fall for the Lord holds them by the hand." He delights in the details. Nothing is too big *or* too small to bring to Him. And He wants to hold your hand every step of the way. Prayer and reading the Word of God are the only things that we can do with lasting effects because they are what God uses to mold and shape us. Only the Lord can change hearts. Not you. Not your intelligence or hard work or perfectly laid out arguments or guilt trips....*any* of it. Only Him. And His change is the kind that lasts.

Sometimes you will get an answer immediately to your prayers and sometimes it will take years, but He *hears* you. And His timing is perfect. I've been praying for two years that we would have more margin in our lives and have "mentioned" it in every way imaginable. Sweetly, not so sweetly, passive aggressively and straight up aggressively. But last night (after really surrendering that same old prayer and idea to God in a passing thought *that morning*), Dom brought up that he doesn't want the business to take so much time away from our family and ministry--out of *nowhere.* He caught me off-guard, but in literally no more than one sentence, I told him I'd been praying for more margin for us in time and finances so we can focus on the truly eternal and important things. He said, "Wow! I really love that! Let's pray about that right now!"

Super-duper not kidding, it's been exactly two years since I brought this up initially, but for some reason last night was the night God chose to align our hearts and give us the same vision in this area. And it was so simple! So beautiful! And took absolutely no prompting or manipulation on my part to get him to see my point of view because God opened his eyes and heart at the time He knew was best. I've been smiling all day remembering the freedom I have to put things in God's hands and that when I take mine off, that's when real change happens. Again, in His timing, not mine. Don't lose faith. Don't get discouraged. Know that He heard your prayer and He is working on it and thank Him in advance that He will answer it whenever and however He sees fit. He's a good Father. He's a sovereign God. He is working all things out for good in your life. Keep praying. Write prayers down. Talk out loud. Sing to Him. 1 Thessalonians 5:16-18 says, "Rejoice always, pray without ceasing, give thanks in all circumstances; for this is the will of God in Christ Jesus for you."

The last thing I want to mention is Philippians 2:3: "Don't be selfish; don't try to impress others. Be humble, thinking of others as better than yourselves." This seems like a totally different topic but I think it goes hand-in-hand when it comes to our hearts when we pray. Do you think of yourself as better than your spouse? Do you think his sin is worse than yours? I'm going to pop your bubble because it's not. Kate and I are doing this study about Joseph called Forgiveness by Melissa Spoeslstra and one of the things she says is that "we tend to judge others by their actions but ourselves by our intentions."[1] Are you extending to him the same grace you extend to yourself? Or better yet, the same grace Christ extends to you? How are your conversations with your husband? What is your tone like? Are you judging him constantly?

This week I want you to ask God once again to give you eyes to see your husband the way He sees them. Satan wants you to view him in a negative, unforgiving way. He wants to accuse him through you. Don't be his vessel! Be the Lord's vessel. Ask Jesus to fill you with His Spirit and let your words, your texts, your calls, and your actions bring life to him, not death. When you see him correctly, as a beloved child created by the God of the Universe, someone for whom Christ died, your prayers will be more effective because you're praying from a place of truth and proper perspective.

Heavenly Abba, we thank You that You want us to come to You with the big things and the small things. I love that when we come to You, You hear us and that Your timing on the answer will always impress us with Your perfection. Please replace the lie that Satan often puts in our head that our prayers don't work. We know from Your Word that prayer is one of the most effective and powerful things we can do. It protects our minds, it cultivates our relationship with You and it is part of Your strategy in the war that goes on in the heavenlies. We pray You would grow our desire to know You more and talk with You more about even the smallest of details, because You truly care. It's in Jesus' name we pray, since He is the reason we can boldly approach Your throne, Amen.

PART TWO
HOW TO START YOUR OWN GROUP

THE FIRST STEPS

THE RULES

THE EMAILS

THE MEETINGS

DEALING WITH EMERGENCIES AND CASUALTIES

TESTIMONIALS

APPENDIX: WISDOM FROM FELLOW WARRIOR WIVES

RECOMMENDED RESOURCES

NOTES

FIRST STEPS

As you embark on this new journey of beginning a group of Warrior Wives, your very first step is to pray! Pray that the Lord would lead you and bless you as you seek Him to strengthen your marriage and the marriages of the women who will join you. Pray also that He would put women on your heart and in your path to invite to join. Remember this is not exclusive! You want to keep this open to anyone who desires to start praying more for their husband — the more varied the group the better. You want to make sure you have varied ages in the group and marriages of different lengths if possible. Titus 2:3-4 states the importance of older women training younger women. In one of my favorite meetings we ever had, a woman who had been married for almost forty years was encouraging the younger women with small children that this stage was especially difficult and that it gets easier. The group let out a collective sigh of relief! It's important to seek the wisdom and counsel of women whose marriages have weathered the test of time. We have never kept the group exclusive and encourage one another to invite other women in their lives to join. So many of the women in our group I had never had the privilege of meeting prior to one of my friends reaching into their *own* circle and extending the invitation. You never know who might need this in their life. One of my greatest blessings so far has been getting to know new friends whose hearts are also led to stand for their marriages in prayer.

Your next step is to prayerfully seek a co-leader. Within the first two years of this group I had two babies seventeen months apart. There were definitely a couple of meetings I could not attend and having Kate there for me was a huge relief. Sickness, family emergencies, vacations, LABOR (ha!), etc. happen and you want the monthly meetings to be consistent so others can count on them.

Third, you will want to find a location and establish a time. The meeting doesn't have to take place at the same home every single time but again, for the sake of consistency, it's best to try and have it in the same location. Kate and I chose to do the first Wednesday of every month from 6:30-8:30p.m. I would always send an email the week before, and on the day of our meeting I would post a reminder in our private Facebook group which I will go into more detail about later.

Fourth, you want to invite women to join! In the introduction, I gave you a sample invitation email that you can use verbatim or just as an example to give you an idea. You want to make this personal and possibly include why you want to start this group. Ask for them to respond if they are interested and then begin compiling a list of emails (I do this in the notes section of my phone) that you can quickly access each Monday when you send out the weekly email. Throw a date out there with a location and see if that works for the majority of those interested and if not, consider a different day of the week. The number of women is up to you but from my experience, the group *will* grow so definitely give it room to do just that.

Next, set reminders in your calendar on your phone and computer until sending out weekly emails and reminders becomes a habit for you. I'm a bit sleep deprived from three rowdy boys so calendar alerts are my friend! Well, calendars and coffee. Yes, please. I have an alarm in my phone to remind me to send the email every Monday. I have another one a week before our meeting on the first Wednesday of the month, in addition to one on the actual meeting day. And I have *another* one to remind me to gather prayer requests on the first of each month so that they can be sent out in one of the first Monday emails of that month. This might seem excessive but you know yourself and what you will need to do to stay on top of this. Just remember that your faithfulness to being steadfast and consistent every week and month will be a determining factor in whether or not this group lasts through the year (and hopefully beyond!). Your members won't invest if they don't feel you are invested. As wives, mothers, workers, leaders and volunteers (among the many other hats we wear!), other things are constantly vying for our attention and unfortunately, we often let these things take priority over our marriages. This group is designed to keep our marriages fresh on our minds by encouraging truth, accountability and prayer. By setting the tone that you are able to be counted on and that you strongly believe our marriages deserve to be second place on our priority list (right below God), members will feel safe to lean into this and devote the time because they will quickly see how imperative it is in their lives.

Finally, send that first email! You will find fifty-two emails in part one, one for each week of the year. That first email (after your invitation email) will include details about the group meeting, the rules of the group (see section labeled "Rules") and your first encouragement to them about their marriages. This is your group so please feel free to replace any email along the way with a personal testimony from yourself, or someone in the group, or something you've stumbled on that you think would inspire your members. Or use the book as a group devotional and you can send an email discussing each week in your own words. Make it personal, biblical and transparent in a way that does *not* dishonor your husband and you will find your members feeling encouraged and safe to be transparent as well.

THE RULES

Before we look at the guidelines, let's revisit the theme of the *Warrior Wives Club* to understand why they are important: **The Warrior Wives Club exists to learn biblical truths to strengthen us to become "a wife of noble character" and to give us a safe community to fight for our marriages through the power of prayer.** These rules are set up to protect the integrity of the group and to avoid at all costs a gossip circle or a place where it's acceptable to "husband bash."

RULE 1: What happens in *Warrior Wives Club* stays in *Warrior Wives Club*: transparency is encouraged but only because it's a safe environment. You will be loved on and prayed for and you will not be exposed or gossiped about. What you share stays there.

RULE 2: Never shame or uncover your husband. Speak with respect about him the way you would want him to speak about you.

RULE 3: Commit to not only praying for your spouse, but the other marriages as well when requests go out each month.

In the two and a half years this group has existed, we have not had one incident where a confidence was breached or where slander has taken place. I believe we have avoided this for two reasons: The lavish grace of God and the rules we set for the group. They are simple but they are important. They also need to be repeated throughout the year. A tactful way I've found to do that is when a new member joins, welcome her to the group in a weekly email and then repeat the rules. Express that it's not only for her benefit but is a refresher for everyone because the adherence to those rules will be the life or death of your group.

By adhering to these rules and encouraging the others of their importance, you will have a safe place for women to truly share their hearts without fear. When truth is allowed to come out in a loving environment where scripture is the ultimate authority
, true change can begin to take place.

THE EMAILS

Every Monday, I have an alarm on my phone that reminds me to send a "Warrior Wives" email. By sending the email on Monday, you are setting a tone for their week and reminding them to look at their marriage and their husband through God's eyes. With all of the demands in life, it's easy to let our marriages take a backseat with the thought that you can always prioritize it later. Yet when we have intentionally put our priorities in the right order (God first, marriage second, kids, ministry or work in whichever order applies to your situation), everything else goes smoothly and harmoniously, the way it was intended. One member said that even if she doesn't have time to read the email right away, it's still a much needed reminder to put her marriage before her kids and work.

As mentioned before, you should have a collection of email addresses for the members of your group somewhere easily accessible to you. Mine is kept in the "Notes" app of my phone, but you can also set up a list within your email account or use an app that you are comfortable with. As new members join, make sure to continually update that list.

At whatever time you decide, send out the weekly email by copying the content from the digital format which will be provided for you by emailing ashbyduval@gmail.com. Some weeks you may be inspired to use something else like a biblically sound encouragement from a marriage centered blog, article, sermon, or something personal from your own life. Something that has been a huge blessing is to ask other women in your group to share their own testimony or lessons learned in marriage. By encouraging the other members to participate in the weekly emails, you will learn more about them and gain invaluable insight. One of the devotionals in the appendix of this book in relation to finances in marriage is from a wife in our group who has been a financial advisor for years. She could speak directly to this subject in such an amazing way because she has seen it ALL! Encouraging them to share their own experiences involves them at a deeper level and blesses the others with their wisdom.

Before ending your email (especially the ones getting close to your next meeting), you will also want to update them on when and where the next meeting will take place. I always include the time and address in case there is someone who has never attended before.

Once a month, you will collect and compile prayer requests in whichever platform you are most comfortable with and then send them out in the following weekly email. This will be the most time consuming part of your role as leader but it is also the most important. At the beginning of the month in a weekly email right after the devotional/encouragement, I ask everyone to reply to that email with their requests. In my experience, only a few women will do this. Most mean to but they want to think about their request first and before they know it, the week has passed them by. So, I give them until Friday, then I go through my list and send a simple text to each member asking them if they have a request for that month. This is actually vital to making sure no one falls through the cracks. There is such a blessing in touching base with each woman, not only for you but for them. It provides a way to stay in touch despite the busyness of life and is a wonderful way to remind them they are cared for and loved. In addition, some of the most serious requests ever received would have never been known had it not been for the text messages.

Once they reply, copy and paste the request into a new note (or app of your choice) and once they are all compiled, copy and paste them into a new email the following Monday with the month and subject (ie: "April Prayer Requests"). It's a good idea to include some sort of reminder that this is the most important aspect of the group and to please take the time to pray over each request and to keep them within the group.

Another way to do prayer requests is by partnering up the women for the month so each person has a prayer partner they can reach out to at any point. To pair them off, I printed off the names of each woman, cut them into strips and put them in a ziplock bag and drew randomly. I then texted each pair their respective info and encouraged them to reach out that day with a prayer request to their partner and to periodically encourage one another throughout the month. This was a huge hit with the women and allowed them to get to know one another better.

In conclusion, the emails are an extremely substantial part of this group because you will have ladies who will never make it to a single meeting or who are only able to make it sporadically. There might be schedule conflicts or members who live in completely different cities, states (or even countries!) and the group meeting is not a pre-requisite to being a part of the group. I do not want to understate how incredible these meetings are, but do not let their inability to come prohibit them from being a part of the *Warrior Wives Club* because they will greatly benefit from the emails and praying for one another via the monthly prayer requests.

THE MEETINGS

Once a month, we get together for a *Warrior Wives Club* meeting for around two hours. You can meet more than that but we had a lot of moms with young kids and many women who were already in a small group with their church so this seemed to work best. We picked the first Wednesday of the month to keep it easy to remember and tried to keep it in the same location. I wouldn't recommend a public location like a restaurant or coffee shop because you want a safe space where people can share freely and pray without feeling self-conscious. Your home or the home of one of your members tends to work best and because it's once a month, we felt ok with not having kids be allowed at the group. Obviously, if a mother is nursing her infant or there is an emergency you can make exceptions, But again, you want this to be a safe place where everyone can share without distraction and sometimes the topics that come up may not be appropriate for little ears. Also, this gives moms a break at least once a month to put their marriages before their children. We had very simple snacks like a dessert or fruit plate, some lemon ice water and an electric tea kettle readily available with a selection of different hot tea. Simple is key for longevity! Don't overcomplicate anything because to stay the course, you do not want to wear yourself (or your hostess! Thank you Kate!) out.

The format of the meetings has changed over time. In the very beginning, we would try and come up with different topics or questions. Then we tried to go through a study together but not a lot of people would read or be caught up in time for the meeting. We found that this format worked best: A marriage video of some sort (sermons, interviews or a series like *Sacred Marriage* by Gary Thomas or *What did you Expect?* by Paul Tripp) and then a time of discussion, prayer and fellowship. The video was nice because it put everyone on an equal playing field and was a very un-awkward way to get everyone to sit down to begin. It allowed for easy conversation because we could talk about what stood out to us most and there was definitely a plus to not having homework because attendance can be sporadic.

Speaking of attendance, we never knew what to expect! We would have some ladies attend every month without fail, some who came once or twice with several months in the middle and at almost every monthly meeting, we have a new face. This relaxed environment and attitude keeps it open for new members to join in at any point and no one feels like they can't be a part of the group just because they can't make a meeting.

That being said, the meetings rock! They are so encouraging and one woman said it best when she told us that when she left her house, she was yelling at her husband about something and fumed the whole way over. After the meeting, she walked into the house and the first thing she did was hug him. To watch a biblically based, marriage-focused video and then to talk and pray about what you are going through with other women, you literally cannot leave there without feeling hope. You feel less alone because so many are facing similar sin issues in their own hearts or similar marriage frustrations. Now be forewarned, Satan will try and discourage you from making these meetings. I started the darn thing, made almost every meeting for two years so I KNOW how amazing they are and yet without fail, every month, I find myself not wanting to go. I feel too tired or not in the mood to socialize or can think of a bunch of other things I feel like I "should" be doing. But this is from the enemy! He doesn't want you to go to strengthen your marriage and will try and keep you from it. Fight the urge to bail and just go! And encourage your members to do the same. You won't be sorry. And your husband will be so thrilled with the mood you come home in that he will make it a point encourage you to go and to clear his schedule to watch the kids for you if that's the season you're in.

DEALING WITH EMERGENCIES AND CASUALTIES

We have a lot of success stories from the last couple of years but I would be remiss if I didn't include that we also had two marriage casualties. THIS CLUB WILL NOT SAVE YOUR MARRIAGE. Only Jesus can do that! But prayer is very powerful and praying with others even more so. A long time ago a woman who had been married for fifty years told me that if you are married for any length of time, the thought of divorce will go through your head. No one is immune to the enemy's assault on our marriages or the selfishness in our flesh that we have to die to regularly. But I strongly believe there is no marriage that cannot be saved. The Lord can resurrect the dead so He can also resurrect your dead marriage. Will it be easy? Heck no! It will be the hardest fight of your life! But you do not have to white-knuckle this thing alone. First of all you have a God that never leaves you or forsakes you, and being a part of a group gives you women who will keep praying when you run out of strength to utter the words.

That being said, there is a good chance someone in your group will experience adultery, addiction, apathy or abuse at some point and you need to be prepared. The first thing is to ask your church, or someone you trust, for local biblical counselor references. You are not a counselor and no one is expecting you to be. As a leader, however, you want to have the information readily available should something come up. In the "Resource" section in the back of the book, you will find options for online counseling and resources for spouses dealing with addiction. You will find resources for women choosing to stand for their marriages despite infidelities as well.

Another good practice that helps if something urgent pops up in a marriage between meetings is to send an emergency email or make a private facebook update to the group. The private Facebook group is nice for not only emergencies but uplifting scriptures, quotes and stories as well throughout the week. Here is an example of one such facebook post and emergency email:

EMERGENCY PRAYER REQUEST
Dear Warrior Wives,

The very reason we gather either physically or in the Spirit is to pray for the Lord to intervene in our marriages and to change our hearts and our husbands hearts so that our marriages could not only survive, but thrive.

Tonight we have a wife in our group who is hanging on by a thread in her marriage and is desperate for help. Her husband has been struggling with pornography and masturbation on and off their entire marriage. It greatly affects their intimacy and often breaks her heart. She needs divine intervention for him to truly turn from this bondage and wisdom on what to do. Also for him to truly see the damage this is causing not only himself but his family and that Jesus would give him the strength to truly turn from this.

Please, please, please lift her up tonight. And if you are able, would you consider fasting and praying at some point this week? It doesn't have to be food. It can be sugar, caffeine, social media, TV, whatever. Over and over in scripture the power of fasting and praying (especially together with other believers) is cited. Just take whatever time you would normally devote to whatever you are fasting from and pray instead.

This is why we exist. To lift each other up when we no longer have the strength to go it alone. To not feel alone in our fight to stay married but to have women who will stand with you to fight the good fight, shoulder to shoulder. Our enemies are not against flesh and blood so we must not fight with flesh and blood weapons but the weapons the Lord gives us in Ephesians 6 which are His word and prayer.

Thank you for kneeling before our Father with me tonight,
Ashby

Sometimes despite everything, you will experience a casualty of divorce. Should you experience a marriage casualty in the group, keep reaching out to her. She will be dealing with more pain in her life than ever before. You don't want to have any other agenda than to simply love her and be there for her. And keep praying! There are so many instances where divorces can turn around and the couple get re-married. No marriage is ever hopeless!

I hope you feel equipped to start your own group having read this content. You will not be leading this alone! First and foremost, Jesus never leaves you or forsakes you and will give you the strength and grace you need every step of the way. Second, please use me as a resource! I will be happy to respond to you with any questions you have. I'm not an expert on marriage but I can say my marriage is infinitely better as a result of regularly praying with other warriors for my husband. And yours will be too! God bless you as you start this life changing group and fight for the most important human relationship you will have on this earth!

TESTIMONIALS

If it weren't for the encouragement of the other warrior wives, this book would not be in your hands. It has been an amazing two and a half years of growth, love, tears and laughter. Here are some of their experiences in their own words.

"Being a part of this group has been life changing, not necessarily because we focus on marriage but that we focus on Jesus and prayer! I've been reminded by our meetings and regular uplifting emails that if I'm having problems with my husband or my marriage, it's a heart issue. Whether his or mine (or both), this heart issue can only be addressed by connecting to Jesus. So what can I do for my marriage? I can focus on my relationship with Jesus, and since I cannot change my husband, I can pray for him diligently while intentionally show respect for him. Plus, having a network and support of like-minded prayer warriors, I am reminded that I am not alone in this battle and we fight together!"
-Sarah

"I really never realized how important it was to be praying daily for just my husband until our marriage was wrecked to the core and tested by Satan in a way I had never been personally tested. It was through a combination of Recovery ministry and a dependency to surround myself with a group of woman that would encourage and build up the high priority of praying for the one the Lord has chosen for me regardless of our circumstances. I'm thankful for this encouraging ministry and the group that it represents. Thanks for your diligence, please continue sharing!"
-Amber

"I have to tell you how much I always look forward to getting an email from you every week, and the warrior wives meetings! I have always gotten so much out of them, to wholeheartedly apply in my marriage. Thank you very much for your willingness and faithfulness in serving the Lord this way."
-Carolina

"Warrior Wives Club is an authentic group of wives I lean on and learn from. We trust, respect, and care for one another and our marriages. Most importantly we keep biblical truth at the center and foundation of our conversations. I am very grateful for the prayers, authenticity, and spiritual support."
-Terren R.

"I was filled with joy when I saw that you were taking our group's compilations of emails and putting them together as a book. You have been an encouragement to me from afar and so many other women. I truly believe you have no idea the number of lives you have touched. Your writings are more than emails, they are weekly gifts of encouragement from the Holy Spirit through you. I believe this. I felt that you needed to know this and I wanted to congratulate you again on this amazing accomplishment. I will be one of the first to purchase this beautiful book."
-Jessica

"WWC offers the encouragement and support we all need to thrive in our marriages. It's an environment to share our weaknesses, celebrate our successes."
-Drea

"The Holy Spirit is so good to use Ashby's weekly encouragements as timely reminders of how I can apply Biblical principals to my marriage. The honesty and transparency of our group is refreshing and knowing that we fervently pray for one another gives me peace in times of need. The world today has demonized the Biblical concepts of submission and servitude in marriage. Having a group of women who believe in and trust in God's plan for marriage makes me feel less crazy and serves as a reminder that Biblical marriages are worth fighting for!"
-Brooke

"When we started this group, I really thought my prayers would change things in my husband. What I didn't realize was how much my prayers would change ME. Ashby and I joke often we aren't sure if anyone else is getting anything out of this group but we sure needed it and it's definitely made OUR marriages a lot better!"
-Kate

APPENDIX: WISDOM FROM OTHER WARRIOR WIVES

APPENDIX 1
MONEY AND MARRIAGE
By *Michelle Minisci*

Growing up in Naples with a single mom, I began to hate people with money. I never understood how a Christian could own a large home without guilt. Then God taught me some lessons about this when my mentor in high school was a doctor's wife and I learned what happens to a doctor after a large malpractice suit: he loses everything but their home. So my friend/mentor owned a large home so they could sell it and start over with money for their young family if needed. For it is not money that is evil, but the *love* of money (1 Timothy 6:10). God uses money all the time. He especially uses it to check our idols. We all have them. I always say that more money means more responsibility.

Fast forward and these lessons and tough questions I asked Christians with money led me to study finance in college. I said out loud to God that I would *never* become a financial advisor. And sure enough, I was offered a job as a financial advisor right out of college and I am still in the same firm (12 years now). I am now a Certified Financial Planner and I love working with our clients!

I have learned many things from our clients and I usually come home to Marc talking about hard lessons I hope we can avoid! This includes a time when we were engaged and I was working closely with a spouse caring for her dying husband and I asked Marc if he would do all that for me (poor Marc--but he puts up with me!).

We believe a few things in our firm. We believe husbands and wives make better decisions together than apart. Most of the time one spouse handles the family finances but we still encourage both spouses to meet with us when large decisions are made or to review their overall financial plan. Also, we believe spenders marry savers and vice versa. Most people think I am a saver but in my marriage, I am the spender. I have to force Marc to even buy a $12 belt! We also believe in joint finances or at least no secrets when it comes to finances. People may have their reasons for separating finances (like a late in life second marriage) but most of the time it is not advisable.

Though my partner is also a Christian, most of the above is not directly from the Bible but life experiences. There are actually a ton of verses on money in the Bible. God talks more about money than heaven and hell combined! (See more about that here: https://www.biblemoneymatters.com/bible-verses-about-money-what-does-the-bible-have-to-say-about-our-financial-lives/) In my career, I see Matthew 6:21 lived out all the time: "For where your treasure is, there your heart will be also." Early on in my career, we had a widow with $8 mil and she said she would lie awake at night worrying if she would have enough money to live on. That was crazy to me. Still is, but now I understand that her money was her treasure and she could not see past it. This happens in church when people give money: they think this gives them the authority to dictate how that money is spent. It is called a gift. It is not your money but God's. God doesn't need your money. If you say no, He will find another way, and that person will be blessed by being used by God. We can't help but attach our heart to our treasure so my challenge to myself is to give when God says, "Give." And allow my heart to find joy in what God does with His "treasure."

Marriage is based on trust and maybe because I married a saver, it's easy for me to trust him but he needs to trust me. It might be easy for me to hide things since he doesn't look at things the way I do. Or maybe it would be easy not to take the time to explain something to him so that he can pray about a decision and give his input. Most of my clients are older when their spouse dies so I take this as a learning opportunity to teach Marc about finances. Some widows/widowers are left not knowing the first thing about handling the finances (that is the late spouse's fault in my opinion). Or the other spouse over complicated it (guilty!). Marc even admitted to forgetting how to use a debit card after we got married. It happens but don't stop including your spouse. Take the time. Some people even recommend a "money date" where you sit down at some predetermined frequency to discuss your family finances.

If you are married to a spender, you may need to have the conversation about trust first, then apply it to your finances. Proverbs 19:1 said, "Better is a poor person who walks in his integrity than one who is crooked in speech and is a fool." Or Proverbs 10:9, "He who walks in integrity walks securely, but he who perverts his ways will be found out." Another tip is to have a set amount, that if one of you wants to buy something over say $100 that you have to discuss it and both agree before proceeding. This still gives flexibility to the spouse that does not control the finances to spend money at Starbucks or something small that is under the pre-set amount. And it gives accountability to the one controlling the finances, like a checks and balances system.

Which brings me to the last item: joint accounts. I do not see any reason why you should have a separate checking account from your spouse. When I hear about it and start delving in, it is most often about trust. Most recently, it was a saver who controlled the finances and had a "secret savings" in her name only so that her husband didn't spend it. No. So wrong. This needs to be disclosed, talked about and trust needs to be addressed. If he can't be trusted with spending, then she can't be trusted because she is hiding. I also know of another couple where the wife had large student loans from her master's degree and he had a golf membership - all before marriage. So they decided to keep with their financial plans before marriage and kept things separate instead of bringing everything to the table to figure out if the golf membership was still a good idea in their new relationship. Communication. Vulnerability. Letting your spouse have an opinion about how you spend money. These are all hard but required to cement your lives together under God's plan.

Another issue is balance. Some say to give away all your possessions. And if that is what God is calling you to do, then say yes and let God handle the consequences! I advise our clients to have 3-6 months income saved in an easy to reach place. Then you have the parable of the rich fool in Luke 12 which talks about storing your treasure in places thieves and moths will destroy. And yes, with the state of our current economic system, your 401(k) will fluctuate in value, but Proverbs 27:12 (NLT) says, "A prudent person foresees danger and takes precautions. The simpleton goes blindly on and suffers the consequences." God also wants us to have balance and be wise. Your emergency savings are still not yours but God's and he will spend it as he sees fit. Though I would have loved a Hawaiian vacation - God's plan was to spend almost all of our emergency savings on surgery for our youngest son Jude. It's His money. All of it. Not just 10%.

The balance is in your trust in God to take care of you and your family. Your emergency savings or lack thereof should not determine your peace but God alone. Only He can give you this peace. Trust me, it does not matter how much money our clients have! Peace comes from God, not money. Look more into the parable in Luke 12: the rich man is considered a fool because while he was planning and building a new place to store his crop, God knew he would die that night! You do not know the plans God has for you. Your heart matters more than your bank account. Your marriage matters more than your bank account. Your kids matter more than your bank account.

There is a reason that Martin Luther talked about three needed conversions: Heart, Mind and *Purse*. It is hard. It is usually the last thing for you to surrender before God or to surrender to your spouse. Certainly it is not surrendered before marriage. And any time that it is, it causes conflict, because you are not under the sanctity of marriage. It is also the first step a spouse acts on that starts to divide a marriage. A marriage that does not hide financial decisions, that discusses all, that trusts the other in their decisions (or trusts the Holy Spirit inside their spouse), that is the kind of marriage that God designed. I am praying for all of you as you may need to surrender your purse before God and your spouse.

APPENDIX 2
EXPOSED
By Kim Shepson

In my heart, I'm a mountaineer. In reality, I'm a midwestern mom. Although I've tasted summit glory on a small scale, I've recently enjoyed reading books about attempted ascents of Denali, K2, and Everest. Truth be told, the most interesting books detail summit failures. In my binge reading of climbing books, more than one poor soul was blown off a ridge of the mountain by a fierce wind or falling rock. Each climber faced complete exposure to a storm, avalanche, or severe weather without having adequate protection or shelter. They were vulnerable.

We don't have mountains in the Midwest, but I've encountered a good number of women who feel just as vulnerable. On their journey through life, they thought they had the formidable protection of marriage—a strong marriage that would offer shelter through any storm. But time and stress, demands and jobs, children and…so many things…erode the foundation of a marriage and threaten its stability. Our marriages should be rock solid fortresses. But sometimes they feel more like a tattered tent being torn by the winds of adversity.

Walking the dangerous ridge of a cold relationship, many women are left vulnerable to—of all things—kindness. The kindness that comes from an interested stranger or friend with a listening ear. Female infidelity has reportedly increased, not because women stop loving their husbands, but because they don't feel like they receive attention, time, and genuine care from them. Like a dry sponge, women thirst for love and affirmation and are sometimes willing to soak it up from any source.

Most marriages will go through difficult seasons of weakness and vulnerability, leaving spouses momentarily exposed to outside pressures and temptations that prevail against them. How do we stay the course in our journey to glorify God, and strengthen our marriages in order to lessen the impact and intensity of intermittent 'exposure'?

First, as women, we need to seek God foremost for His love, support, and protection. Our marriages should provide these elements, but they aren't perfect. Only God is. Sometimes we look to our spouses for the security, consistency, and love that only God can provide. David writes, "The Lord is my rock, my fortress and my deliverer; my God is my rock, in whom I take refuge" (Psalm 18:2). We can trust in the dependability of God, and we need to look to Him first to meet our needs.

Second, pray for your husband and your marriage. Pray for your communication and your ability to understand one another. Men bear a lot of pressure to provide and be the perfect husband and parent. Pray for him. God can do more in our husbands' hearts than we could ever accomplish through our words. And in prayer, God often softens our own hearts and rids them of selfishness and sin.

Third, surround yourself with godly women. If you are already saturated with love and encouragement from sisters in Christ, you will less likely soak up and seek kindness from another man. Every person faces temptation—even Jesus was tempted in the wilderness. Temptation isn't sin—but it can most certainly lead to it. Peter writes in I Peter 5:8, "Your enemy the devil prowls around like a roaring lion looking for someone to devour." Just as a lion will stalk a weak lamb separated from the flock, the evil one will seize the opportunity to prey upon and tempt a person when they're alone and lonely.

Fourth, repair broken walls. Nothing is more healing to a relationship than a sincere, humble, and generous apology. And be willing to receive one. Paul writes, "Forgive as the Lord forgave you" (Colossians 3:13).

Fifth, build your marriage with kindness. Kindness is love lived out. Paul teaches us to build others up according to their needs and to be kind and compassionate to one another (Ephesians 4:29,

32). A while ago, I decided to self-impose a Kindness Project for one month, where I would intentionally try to go out of my way to do and say kind things for my husband. I kept a journal to see if anything changed in our relationship. First of all, I changed. My heart changed. But my husband changed too. He seemed less on-guard and more kind as a result. And after one week he asked me on a date—I couldn't remember the last time that had happened.

Finally, guard where you go—and where you allow your mind to go. We often aren't surprised where temptation lurks—our biggest surprise might be how much we're attracted to it. James writes, "Resist the devil, and he will flee from you. Come near to God and He will come near to you" (James 4:7-8).

Even in the best marriages, there will be times when our relationships aren't as strong as they should be. It's especially in times of vulnerability, when we feel alone and exposed to the pressures and temptations of the world, that we need to seek shelter in God, find comfort in the warmth of Christ-centered fellowship, and work to repair brokenness. God can renew and strengthen our marriages so that they provide support and protection for us through all of life's pressing storms.

Great marriages don't just happen. We have to nurture them, protect them, and fight to keep them on-course.

APPENDIX 3
MIRACLE MORNING MARRIAGE
By Dora Watson

Six weeks ago, I challenged myself to make a life change. I wanted to see what would happen if I put down my electronics and social media (at least most of the time!!), and instead picked up books and more productive habits. And I wanted to see what would happen if, for a year, I acted as if everything the Bible says is true. Of course, as a Christian, I have always theoretically believed everything in the Bible is true ("All Scripture is inspired by God and profitable for teaching, for reproof, for correction, for training in righteousness;" 2 Timothy 3:16), but I definitely haven't acted on the parts that I found more convenient to ignore. So to start this new challenge, I started waking up an hour earlier, and the first book I read was *Miracle Morning* by Hal Elrod, which is all about getting up and creating a really productive, goal-oriented morning that helps lead to more productive days.

For a week, I woke up at 6am and read, meditated/prayed, journaled and occasionally jogged or walked. After a week, my non-morning-person husband decided to join me. So for the last five weeks (with a break when we had colds), we have been getting up together at 6am, drinking our coffee, reading and working on ourselves, together, for an hour. We each focus on our own goals, but we take time to chat about what we are reading, laugh, and enjoy the time we have without distractions. It has been such a blessing to our relationship, and to my own personal happiness. Will and I have quality, productive time together every day, and I have the opportunity to work on my own goals, which I think often get left behind when we are so busy being wives and moms. I feel like I have a small little sliver of control over my day, and because of intentional time in prayer and reading, I feel like my spiritual life is gradually improving too.

I am excited to see the results that come of this after a year!

APPENDIX 4
WHO CAN YOU TALK TO IN A CONFLICT
Anonymous Group Member

God joined a man and woman together in marriage so together they would mirror His image. Oneness reflects the character and unity of God (Matthew 19:4-6; John 17:22-23).

Ashby asked me to share a promise my husband and I made to each other about oneness in our marriage. When there is a conflict between my husband and I, we promise to solve it between each other and if outside help is needed, we will go to a pastor, Christian counselor, or a mutual person we both respect and trust. Individually we can talk with someone we trust, but not family, not all my girlfriends or all my husband's guy-friends, and if a very serious conflict arises, preferably not girlfriends or guy-friends we both know and do things with; this can make one or both of us feel very awkward when we get together with them. The intention of talking with someone must be to seek help and support; not to just complain or tell on your spouse for the sole purpose of hurting them. Reaching out to a private group, like this one, that honors and respects privacy for prayer or advice is okay. If a very serious conflict arises, we promised to reach out anonymously. A month or so ago Ashby emailed an emergency prayer request. My husband and I had experienced a similar situation in our marriage. Before sharing our personal marriage experience with the group, I asked my husband if he was okay with me sharing it.

First reason we made this promise: oneness requires putting your marriage and spouse before yourself. Before making any decision, it is important to stop and think, is this decision putting my marriage and spouse's needs first? This requires a total shift from our natural selfishness of only thinking about ourselves. This concept applies even if your spouse hurts you and you want to lash out and hurt him back.

Second reason: oneness requires complete trust in the other person. If we both know our marriage is held sacred, our relationship will grow. If I know my husband is telling everything bad I do with his mom, guy-friends, etc., it breaks my trust and thus oneness will not be achieved.

Third reason: if I share something bad my husband did with my mom, I may have no problem forgiving him, but my mom may not be able to forgive him. She doesn't get to hear my husband and I talk, apologize, etc. This will affect how my mom thinks about my husband and how she treats him. This can then snowball and affect my husband's desire to spend time with my family, etc.

One particular conflict during our 24 year marriage almost ended our marriage. We both didn't know if we wanted to stay married. With the promise we made to one another regarding oneness in mind, this is how we handled our conflict...

I cried and screamed out to God until I had nothing to cry and scream about. Soon after this complete collapse before God, I had the most comforting feeling come over my entire body that everything was going to be okay; I didn't know if it meant leaving my husband or staying, but I knew either way I would be okay. I knew this comfort was from God. I held onto that comfort as tight as I could for the months to come. I also paid close attention to any signs God was telling me about what to do. For example, one day I got the feeling I should turn on the radio. I generally do not listen to the radio during the day; I generally only listen when I am driving. When I turned on the radio, the pastor seemed to be talking directly to me about my current situation. I knew God had me turn on the radio at that very second. God also made me aware of Family Life's "A Weekend to Remember" marriage conference; I had never heard of it before then.

I sought counsel from a priest a few times. I later worked with a pastor's wife. I only told one friend what was going on. I felt it was okay to tell her given she lived in a different state and she didn't have any contact with my husband. I listened to a lot of Christian talk radio and sermons, read the Bible and other resources, and I reached out to my Christian friends asking them to pray for my husband and I as we were struggling but I never gave them any details of what was going on. I never told my family what was going on and it was really, really hard not to tell my mom. But, to this day I am so happy I didn't. It would have affected what they think of my husband and how they treat him. To this day my husband is very grateful he doesn't have to walk on eggshells around them.

Over the next few months, God moved in beautiful ways with my husband too. Thankfully we both agreed to attend Family Life's "A Weekend to Remember" marriage conference. It gave us the tools and knowledge we needed. We both wish we had known about this conference long ago. Our marriage was transformed and I am so happy to say our marriage is beautiful today! At the time, our conflict seemed impossible to overcome and was horrifically painful, but I look back now and as weird as this may sound, I am grateful it happened. This hurtful and painful conflict saved our marriage and we now have a beautiful marriage because of it.

Some couples are very transparent about their conflicts, e.g., I have listened to many couples on Christian talk radio who go through conflicts and they are open to sharing what happened and what they learned. I am very grateful they can do that as it helped us a lot, but for my husband and I that would tear us apart so we hold our relationship very close.

APPENDIX 5
HOW TO STOP FIGHTING
By Kate Palazzi adapted from
HouseMixBlog.com

Conflict is inevitable in marriage. You have two different genders, with two different upbringings and in our case two different cultures. It's a natural recipe for conflict.[1]

When Marcello and I first moved in together we fought for weeks on end. He moved here for six months from Italy after we had dated two years long distance to basically see if we should get married. I now regret that we lived together before marriage. I had walked so far away from my faith I wasn't sure God existed — a story for another day — and we didn't have too many options as Marcello spoke little English and had no job — also a story for another day! If any two people know about fighting, it's us. We're both passionate and stubborn and half the time we weren't even arguing about the same thing with our language barrier! I didn't know that he would use any and every empty surface on a dresser or table to lay out his things — watch, wallet, anything that belongs in a man purse. He didn't know that I would leave all my shoes by the front door in our tiny apartment. We sat down for dinner and he wanted to know if I had a tablecloth. No. I gave him a placemat. I actually had milk with dinner, like the young midwesterner that I was, which was unacceptable for an Italian. He told me in half English, half Italian that only wine or water was acceptable. Do you see what I'm getting at? We have argued since day one.

Over the last 10 years things have changed. We don't argue about the same things over and over much anymore. We disagree and discuss most things now instead of having a knock-down, drag-out fight. I can't remember the last time I slammed a door or he raised his voice. I'm inviting a challenge from Satan on this, I'm sure, but for the most part we talk things out together in detail until we're blue in the face and have reached a compromise or solution. Here are some steps to help you stop fighting:

Be kind

This seems obvious, but I think a lot of us tend to take things out on our spouse instead of building them up and treating them like our other half. How many silly fights could be prevented if we were just nice? I heard someone say once that she wished her husband would treat her as nice as he treats his best friend. It rang in my ears. It resonated with me because I knew that I didn't talk to my husband the way I talked to my best friend.

So I conducted an experiment. For a day, I ran everything I did or said to Marcello through a filter of "would I do or say this to my best friend?" I surprised myself in the worst way. I basically had to eliminate half of my actions and words. No critiquing his parking spot choice. No remarking that the pasta had too much salt in it. No rolling my eyes or giving disapproving looks. Nobody would want a friend who does these things! Why would you want to marry someone who does it on a daily basis? I realized how much work I had to do.I started saying "thank you" for things he did around the house instead of expecting them. "Thanks for remembering to take the trash out on trash days." The quicker I was to show him appreciation, the quicker he was to show me appreciation. It's easier to do the everyday mundane tasks when you know your spouse sees it and is grateful.

It took some brain power to recognize my thought patterns and consciously change them. I saw that when I became aware of and filtered the words that used to flow freely out of my mouth, his behavior changed toward me. As I made an effort to say only things that were true, helpful, inspiring, necessary or kind, he wanted to spend more time with me.

Some sore spots that were once in our marriage began to dissolve. One night I slipped up and began to criticize his dishwashing skills because there was still food on the "clean" dishes. As soon as it came out I regretted it and grit my teeth awaiting his response. To my surprise he laughed and made a joke. Why? Because it had been a long time since he had heard me offer disapproval. Of course, there is a time and place for serious discussion, but here I'm speaking of everyday comments that will hopefully build a partner up rather than tear them down.

Fight fair

When you have an argument with your spouse do you fight to win? Do you think your way is the only right way? Do you keep a mental file cabinet of how you've been wronged? If you do, I have some important news for you: Your spouse is not your enemy. In fact, fighting with your spouse is as futile as a left hand fighting a right hand. You are one, a team who God united as one. Your real enemy is Satan, who wants to destroy your marriage. "For our struggle is not against flesh and blood, but against the rulers, against the authorities, against the powers of this dark world and against the spiritual forces of evil in the heavenly realms" (Ephesians 6:12).

So how can we do battle with our real enemy? Satan is powerful, more powerful than us, but he is only a lion in a cage when we have Jesus. We can call on Christ's authority and omnipotence to overcome our sin and the sin of our loved ones. This is where prayer shakes things up. Doing battle in prayer with God is more effective than 1,000 repeat conversations with your spouse. I really believe that.

Rules during disagreement

Here are some guidelines to a healthy disagreement. Again, think about your tendencies here and pledge to change them.

> Don't fight to win, fight to resolve.
>
> Be respectful.
>
> Don't yell.
>
> Don't interrupt.
>
> Don't bring up past arguments. Discuss the subject at hand.
>
> Don't build a case over time in your mind.

Don't throw or slam things.

Don't cuss.

Don't call names.

Don't be condescending or sarcastic.

Don't play the silent game.

Don't make a low blow to hurt your spouse and "win."

Don't leave the house. If you do, say where you're going and when you'll be back.

Never bring up divorce.

Say you're sorry if you know you're wrong.

Forgive.

When you follow these general rules, the same disagreements don't have to play on repeat. When you don't play fair, you shift the focus to your misbehavior instead of the problem. But when you don't muddy the waters with hurtful comments or condescension, you can focus on the real topic at hand and dig it out from the root so it won't crop up again. Look at your marriage and identify what cycles of disagreement you have taken on. **When you're calm, sit down with your spouse and talk about how you can do it differently, better.** If your arguments are not healthy, what steps can you take? Don't keep doing things the same way and expect different results.

Forgive

If a conflict turns ugly, how can you heal wounds of disappointment and hurt? The answer is forgiveness. Even if he didn't ask for forgiveness.

Why should I forgive? Simply put, because Christ forgives you. Beyond that, the dangers of harboring un-forgiveness toward your spouse (or anyone) are many. Bitterness and resentment take hold and affect your thought patterns, which in turn affect your actions because our actions stem from what is in our heart. If you harbor un-forgiveness in your heart, justify it, relive it, feed it, it will poison you. You might believe you are punishing the person, but you are in fact hurting yourself and blocking God from working in your life. If you're concerned about someone getting away with something if you forgive them, you need to give that to God. As Jesus did, you can trust your case in His hands, who always judges fairly.

The other side of this coin is to ask forgiveness of God and your spouse if you've crossed a line. Humble yourself and say you're sorry for your actions. Name them specifically. Do not say "I'm sorry if I hurt your feelings." Say "I'm sorry I was sarcastic and interrupted you instead of listening to your side."

Compromise and work as a team

Hopefully compromise follows an argument. This doesn't have to have a negative connotation. Compromise doesn't mean you give up, it means you find a middle ground. Some of this might sound like Obvious 101, but some of us really need to hear it, myself included.

Listen and adapt

During a disagreement, do you listen to your mate, or do you plow through and talk over him? You can't just focus on how you've been wronged and the points you want to argue. You also really need to hear what your spouse is saying. Listen to his side so you can find a solution — which will make him much more willing to hear your side too, by the way. Otherwise the argument was for nothing and will most likely come up again.

Or is playing the silent game your secret weapon? Letting things go, or sweeping issues under the rug, will only allow them to fester and grow.

Don't try to change who your spouse is

Somewhere around year seven I noticed that Marcello was perfectly comfortable allowing me to be myself, but I was still trying to make him be like me. I wanted him to do things my way, see things from my perspective, treat people how I would. That's ironic, by the way, because when we walk in the door to a gathering he is greeted with smiles and someone yelling "Marcello!" as if now the party can start. While I'm thrown a courtesy smile and a much more low key, "Hey, Kate." So why I would want to make him just like me when he lights up the room? I'm just not sure.

I had the revelation, as I said, but it has taken time to stop pressing all my insecurities on him, and I'm still not there yet. Did that person know he was joking? Does he know that he should leave more space in between our car and the car in front of us? Does he have to shake his restless leg during the whole church service?

Well, when it boils down to it, I think I just need to get over it. If the person didn't know he was joking, it wasn't my conversation and I'm not accountable for it. He has a driver's license in two countries with no points on either of them and drives all day, every day. He's capable of driving us to Target. And after a decade, I do know that he, in fact, cannot stop shaking his leg and that's ok. I need to let him be who he is.

Talk about expectations

Have you ever been furious at your spouse for something he has neglected? Dirty dishes piled up by the sink, dirty laundry on the floor or kids with unfinished homework? Have you tried asking nicely if he could help? Sometimes we can get so mad about something that we think is glaringly obvious, but it hasn't occurred to our spouse or we haven't even brought it up.

APPENDIX 6
A MARRIAGE COUNSELING EXERCISE
BY EMILY GRAEVE

During one of our final marriage counseling sessions, our counselor had done an exercise with us where we were to write down a couple things we had experienced that day that we wanted to share with our spouse, and how it made us feel. It could be anything on our mind, whether it was an event, an experience we had with God, or something we were feeling. The exercise only took a few minutes and within those few minutes we learned so much about each other that we may not have communicated had we not done this exercise.

The purpose of the exercise was to get us to communicate and have an open discussion each day so that days wouldn't pass where we knew really nothing that our spouse was experiencing. It allowed us to be free and open about ourselves in a way that let our spouse really see into our thoughts and feelings and give them validation. This exercise has prevented many arguments and has been a good ice breaker to initiating things we want to communicate to our spouse in more of a casual loving manner.

Last week when we were doing this exercise before bed, Josh shared his one thing...He explained that the past few weeks had been very draining on him because his boss only points out the things that go wrong and doesn't ever show him praise or encouragement for all that Josh excels at. It has been weighing him down and making him feel like a failure. He mentioned that if his boss could only give a little bit more encouragement for the things he does well on, then it would be so much easier to take the criticism when it comes his way.

As he was explaining this, it opened my eyes to how I need to respond to Josh better as a wife. I forget many times to verbalize all the wonderful ways he is a husband and father in order to fill up his tank, so when the time comes when I need to express my concern about something with him, he then feels like a bad father and husband and his defensiveness kicks in.

Doing this exercise the past few months has been so helpful in seeing a little more clearly into each other's hearts and minds and has prevented many arguments from even occurring. It has allowed someone like me, who is not a communicator, to get a little bit of a push forward to open up to my husband in a more patient and loving manner. So many of our arguments arise because we just have no clue what our spouse is experiencing day in and day out and we just can't seem to figure out a way to communicate it.

This little "one thing" strategy has blessed us tremendously, and I hope it can help all of you too!

RECOMMENDED RESOURCES

Sacred Marriage by Gary Thomas (book and DVD)

What Did You Expect by Paul Tripp (book and DVD)

Love and Respect by Dr. Emerson Eggerichs (book and DVD)

Power of the Praying Wife by Stormie Omartian (book)

The Meaning of Marriage by Tim Keller (book and podcasts)

First Aid for Your Wounded Marriage by Marilyn Philips (a book about standing for your marriage in spite of betrayal)

Married for Life Ministries: biblical coaching and counseling for your marriage
https://www.2equal1.com/courses/courses/married-for-life/

Pure Desire: a resource to help those with sexual addiction
https://puredesire.org

Faithful and True: Christian counseling center specializing in the treatment of sexual addiction for men, support for their spouses, and guidance for couples who have experienced relational betrayal. https://faithfulandtrue.com

GPS Life Journey: a resource to help you see how God has uniquely designed you and your spouse and how to engage in your special roles and God given purpose. http://www.gpslifejourney.com

Focus On The Family: articles and podcasts about marriage.
https://www.focusonthefamily.com/marriage

Stay Married: podcasts to support your marriage.
https://itunes.apple.com/us/podcast/the-staymarried-podcast/id1044136985?mt=2

NOTES

EMAIL 1

1. Stormie Omartian. *The Power of a Praying Wife* (Eugene, Or.: Harvest House, 1997), 17.

EMAIL 2

1. Gary Thomas. *Sacred Marriage* (Grand Rapids, MI: Zondervan, 2000, 2015).

EMAIL 3

1. Revive Our Hearts, https://www.reviveourhearts.com/radio/revive-our-hearts/courage-be-woman/, accessed July 22, 2018.
2. Elisabeth Elliott. *The Path of Loneliness* (Nashville, TN: Thomas-Nelson, 1991), 73.

EMAIL 4

1. *Cinderella Man.* (2005). [DVD] Directed by R. Howard.

EMAIL 6

1. Al-Anon Family Group. *One Day At A Time in Al-Anon* (New York, Al Anon Family Group Headquarters, 1992), 367.

2. Gary Thomas. *Sacred Marriage* (Grand Rapids, MI: Zondervan, 2000, 2015), 86.

EMAIL 7

1. *Sacred Marriage.* (2015). [DVD] Zondervan, session 2
2. *Sacred Marriage.* (2015). [DVD] Zondervan, session 2

EMAIL 8

1. Corrie Ten Boom, *I Stand at the Door and Knock.* (Grand Rapids: Zondervan, 2008), 23.
2. Priscilla Shirer, *The Armor of God.* (Nashville: Lifeway, 2015), 59.

EMAIL 9

1. *Lifeway*, Beth Moore teaching, https://www.lifeway.com/en/product-family/the-patriarchs, accessed August 5, 2018.

EMAIL 10

1. *OnePlace*, Jill Briscoe teaching, http://www.oneplace.com/ministries/telling-the-truth-for-women/listen/queen-of-your-husbands-heart-458677.html, accessed September 21, 2016.

EMAIL 11

1. Elisabeth Elliott. *The Path of Loneliness* (Nashville: Thomas-Nelson, 1991), 158.

EMAIL 13

1. Sarah Mackenzie. *Teaching From a Place of Rest: A Homeschooler's Guide to Unshakeable Peace.* (Camp Hill: Classical Education Press, 2015).

EMAIL 15

1. Mars Hill Church Archive, Mark Driscoll teaching, http://marshill.se/marshill/media/the-peasant-princess, accessed August 29, 2016.
2. iMOM, http://www.imom.com/mismatched-sex-drives-and-what-you-can-do-about-it/#.WyLE4y-ZNmB, accessed August 29, 2016.
3. Libido, Lucy. *Lucy Libido Says.....There's an Oil for*

THAT: A Girlfriend's Guide to   Using Essential
Oils Between the Sheets (1) (Volume 1), (CreateSpace
Independent Publishing Platform; 1 edition, 2016)

.

EMAIL 17

1. The Atlantic, "Master of Love", https://www.theatlantic.
com/health/archive/2014/06/happily-ever-after/372573/
,accessed March 20, 2017.

EMAIL 18

1. **Michael Hyatt,** http://michaelhyatt.com/how-to-become-
your-spouses-best-friend.html, accessed November 10, 2016.

EMAIL 22

1. *Focus on the Family,* http://www.focusonthefamily.com/
media/daily-broadcast/experiencing-a-fulfilled-marriage-pt1,
accessed February 8, 2017.
2. *Psychology Today,* https://www.psychologytoday.com/us/
blog/heart-the-matter/201704/do-half-all-marriages-really-
end-in-divorce, accessed March 12, 2019.
3. *Married For Life,* https://www.2equal1.com, accessed
February 8, 2017

EMAIL 26

1. *To Love, Honor and Vacuum,* http://
tolovehonorandvacuum.com/2012/02/29-days-to-great-sex-
day-27-experiencing-spiritual-intimacy-while-you-make-love/,
accessed August 30, 2016.
2. *Very Well Mind,* https://www.verywellmind.com/why-to-
have-sex-more-often-2300937, accessed August 30, 2016.
3. *What Men Wish Women Knew,* https://youtu.be/
VI17evdc02, accessed August 30, 2016.

EMAIL 27

1. Got Questions, https://www.gotquestions.org/Bible-self-pity.html, accessed September 12, 2018

EMAIL 29

1. *Life Love and Family*, http://www.lifeloveandfamily.org/listen/when-your-husband-is-addicted-to-pornography/, accessed August 23, 2016
2. *Desiring God*, https://www.desiringgod.org/articles/what-if-my-husband-looks-at-porn, accessed August 6, 2018.
3. *Beauty from ashes*, http://beautyfromashes.org/contentpages.aspx?parentnavigationid=298&viewcontentpageguid=4cda8536-69d2-45cb-bbd4-6955e9432e0c , accessed June 14, 2018.
4. *Married for Life Ministries*, https://www.2equal1.com/courses/courses/married-for-life/ accessed August 22, 2016
5. *Pure Desire*, https://puredesire.org accessed August 22, 2016
6. *Faithful and True*, https://faithfulandtrue.com, accessed August 22, 2016
7. *Summit Church*, http://www.recoveryatsummit.com/, accessed August 22, 2016
8. *Covenant eyes*, www.covenanteyes.com, accessed August 22, 2016
9. *X3Watch*, https://x3watch.com/, accessed August 22, 2016
10. *Focus on the Family,* https://store.focusonthefamily.com/5-steps-to-breaking-free-from-porn?visitorid=4b11d6ae-dfa8-4162-b9cc-4ccfa4223195&extra_data=%7B%7D&_ga=2.214906007.1812128998.1529085035-1143620173.1529085035, accessed June 15, 2018.

EMAIL 30

1. Saddleback Church, https://saddleback.com/watch, accessed August 8, 2018.
2. Richard Warren, *The Purpose-Driven Life : What on*

Earth Am I Here for? (Grand Rapids, MI: Zondervan, 2002) Day 19.

3. *Christianity Today*, https://www.todayschristianwoman. com/articles/2015/august/why-controlling-women-kill-relationships.html?start=2 , accessed August 9, 2018.

EMAIL 31

1. Gary D. Chapman, *The five love languages: how to express heartfelt commitment to your mate* (Chicago: Northfield Pub., 1995), 18.
2. Gary D. Chapman, *The five love languages: how to express heartfelt commitment to your mate* (Chicago: Northfield Pub., 1995), p. 19

EMAIL 32

1. *Merriam-Webster*, https://www.merriam-webster.com/ dictionary/vow, accessed September 25, 2018.

EMAIL 35

1. Francis Schaeffer, *The Finished Work of Christ.* (Wheaton: Crossway, 1998), 124.

EMAIL 36

1. *Got Questions*, https://www.gotquestions.org/wives-submit. html, accessed June 18, 2016

EMAIL 37

1. Tim Muehlhoff, *Defending Your Marriage: The Reality of Spiritual Battle* (Downers Grove: IVP Books, 2018).

EMAIL 39

1. *What did you expect? Redeeming the Realities of Marriage.* (2009). Directed by Paul David Tripp. [DVD]. Session 4, Disc 2
2. *Patheos,* http://www.patheos.com/blogs/christiancrier/2015/07/25/top-7-bible-verses-about-unconditional-love/#Oj4m2B0z4QODlVom.99, accessed January 15, 2018

EMAIL 40

1. Gary Thomas. *Sacred Marriage* (Grand Rapids: Zondervan, 2000, 2015), 218-219.

EMAIL 41

1. *What did you expect? Redeeming the Realities of Marriage.* (2009). Directed by Paul David Tripp. [DVD]. Session 9, Disc 4
2. C.S. Lewis, *The Problem of Pain* (New York: Macmillan, 1965), 41.

EMAIL 44

1. *Fierce Marriage,* https://fiercemarriage.com/5-principles-healthier-happier-relationships-laws, accessed March 15, 2018.

EMAIL 45

1. *Tony Evans,* https://tonyevans.org/tony-evans-sermons/, accessed March 27, 2018.

EMAIL 46

1. Philip Yancey, *Prayer: Does It Make Any Difference?* (Grand Rapids, MI: Zondervan, 2006), 166-167.

EMAIL 47

1. *Respectfully Yours.* (2012). Actors Dr. Emerson and Sarah Eggerichs. [DVD]. Session 5, Disc 2.

2. Dr. Emmerson Eggerichs, *Love and Respect: The Love She Most Desires; The Respect He Desperately Needs.* (Nashville: Thomas Nelson, 2004).

EMAIL 52

1. Melissa Spoelstra, *Joseph: The Journey to Forgiveness.* (Nashville: Abingdon Press, 2015), 89.

APPENDIX 1

1. *Bible Money Matters,* https://www.biblemoneymatters. com/bible-verses-about-money-what-does-the-bible-have-to-say-about-our-financial-lives/, accessed August 20, 2017.

APPENDIX 5

1. *House Mix,* http://www.housemixblog.com/2017/08/01/part-2-how-to-stop-fighting-in-your-marriage/, accessed July 23, 2018.

Made in the USA
Monee, IL
28 May 2020